THE
WARRIOR
WITHIN

The philosophies of
BRUCE LEE
to better understand the world around you
and achieve a rewarding life

John Little

CB
CONTEMPORARY BOOKS
A TRIBUNE COMPANY

Library of Congress Cataloging-in-Publication Data

Little, John.
  The warrior within : the philosophies of Bruce Lee to better
understand the world around you and achieve a rewarding life / John
Little ; foreword by Linda Lee Cadwell.
      p.   cm.
  Includes bibliographical references (p.   ) and index.
  ISBN 0-8092-3194-8
  1. Martial arts—Philosophy. 2. Spiritual life. 3. Lee, Bruce,
1940–1973. I. Title.
GV1101.L58   1996
796.8'01--dc20   96-14438
                                                            CIP

Interior design by Frank Loose Design

Published by Contemporary Books, Inc.
Two Prudential Plaza, Chicago, Illinois 60601-6790
Manufactured in the United States of America
International Standard Book Number: 0-8092-3194-8
10   9   8   7   6   5   4   3   2   1

To my wife, Terri, and our children, Riley, Taylor, and Brandon

CONTENTS

FOREWORD

*D*ear Most Fortunate Reader,

Something about Bruce Lee has attracted you to pick up this book. You recall his screen image: a great fighter—fast, powerful—an opponent to be feared; a man in superb physical condition, with washboard abdominals, broad deltoids, defined forearms; an actor whose personality excited you, charmed you, and inspired you. Perhaps you have seen his films many times, classics still unsurpassed in the martial arts genre. But Bruce Lee—a philosopher? This is a side of the man that you haven't considered, but your interest is piqued. Read on, my friend, for within the pages of this book, John Little delivers to you an adventure of the spirit, an opportunity for you to know the *real* Bruce Lee.

During our marriage of nine years, I knew Bruce probably more thoroughly and intimately than most. In his outward life, I saw him struggle to overcome stumbling blocks along the path to the attainment of his goals. In his interior life, I watched him struggle to overcome the self-doubts and insecurities that plague us all. Bruce would be the first person to tell you that he was not a perfect man, but more important, he would say that his mission in life was to become a *real* human being. His journey was a constant process of evolving, one step at a time, with the object being not to reach a state of perfection, but to experience life with every nerve exposed, fully in touch with gut-level feelings and cerebral senses. To this end, Bruce delved deeply into his psyche to define and refine his own philosophy of life.

All knowledge is really self-knowledge, Bruce often said, meaning that the more a person exposes himself to learning opportunities, the more these experiences enrich, enhance, and become part of who that person is. Bruce was a model of a self-educated man. His formal education extended through his junior year at the University of Washington, where he majored in philosophy. When Bruce left college to open the Jun Fan Gung Fu School in Oakland, his education did not stop. Far from it. He continued his quest, the fascination that had driven him from an early age: how does the thinking process of an individual propel him to actualize his full potential in a superior way?

Bruce was determined to learn about this process within himself. Even as he trained his body for strength and efficiency, so did he discipline his mind to search for the causes of his ignorance. So intensely did Bruce focus his attention on this task that his mind became absolutely centered, while at the same time, he was filled with a blazing awareness of all that went on around him—the essential gung fu man. By exploring the depths of his being, he was able to nurture the seeds of his personal philosophy, which grew and blossomed into the *real* Bruce Lee, the man you have experienced as a prodigious fighting machine and that you will now get to know as a philosopher, a man wise beyond his years.

There are others who are good martial artists and fine actors with fabulous physiques. Some have achieved stardom and are richly rewarded for their talent. But there is *something* about Bruce Lee which makes him irreplaceable in the hearts and minds of his followers all over the world. More than two decades after his death, I continue to receive a steady stream of mail from people expressing their admiration for Bruce. A thirteen-year-old young man, born years after Bruce died, writes to tell me how Bruce has motivated him to do well in school; a professional man in his fifties tells me how his life moved in a positive direction because of Bruce's influence; a young woman says she was inspired to study martial arts because of Bruce, and her confidence has soared in all areas of her life. The stories are innumerable, but similar in theme: Bruce Lee is a role model, a hero image, and a *real* human being.

What is this *something* about Bruce Lee that continues to fascinate people in all walks of life? I believe it is the depth of his personal philosophy, which subconsciously, or otherwise, projects from the screen and through his writings. His personality was such that he brought you into his inner world, changed your attitudes, altered your perceptions, fine-tuned your awareness.

This book gives you the opportunity to reshape your memories of Bruce Lee, to view him from a new perspective.

One who has availed himself of the opportunity to learn from Bruce Lee is John Little, author of this book. From an early age, John immersed himself in the study of philosophy and Bruce Lee. Through the application of vast energy and intellect, tireless research, and cultivated insights, John has undertaken to compare and contrast Bruce Lee's philosophy with age-old gurus and modern sages from the East and West. Second, he relates how Bruce applied his philosophy to everyday life and more broadly to his lifelong pursuits. Finally, John opens the door for you to take from Bruce Lee's way of life that which is useful to you, and in so doing, to develop and nurture your own personal philosophy.

To paraphrase one of Bruce's lines from *Enter the Dragon*: "It is like a finger pointing to the moon. Don't concentrate on the finger or you will miss all that heavenly glory." Look beyond the words on these pages. Think about these thoughts, then feel them, then make them your own.

I wish you abundant energy, good health, and quiet awareness.

Linda Lee Cadwell

Linda Lee Cadwell
Boise, Idaho

Postscript: A scholarship in drama has been established in memory and honor of my son, Brandon, at Whitman College. A scholarship for medical research has been established in Bruce and Brandon Lee's names at the University of Arkansas. John Little is donating a substantial percentage of the royalties from the sale of this book to those scholarships. The Lee family is grateful for his generosity.

*T*o the general public, Bruce Lee was a famous Chinese movie star in martial arts films. To the martial arts community, Bruce Lee was a sensational martial artist with superb fighting skills and stage presence who was also the founder of a new fighting system. However, very few people know that Bruce Lee was also an innovative thinker, a philosopher, and a scholar who had a deep understanding of Chinese Taoist and Zen philosophy.

For me, it was a great privilege to become one of his students, training at his Los Angeles school in 1967. Bruce was a master teacher, a creative genius of the twentieth century who was able to combine the ancient philosophy of the *Tao* with a Chinese Wing Chun system, modern Western boxing skills, and karate kicks to create a thoroughly effective unarmed fighting system, which he called jeet kune do (commonly translated into English as "the way of the intercepting fist"), or JKD. His teachings have awakened in me a new understanding of the ultimate reality in unarmed combat and have totally altered not only my training, but my whole life.

Bruce Lee's thoughts and writings regarding his JKD philosophy were printed in many publications over a period of some sixteen years. Some of these periodicals have long since vanished from existence, which has made it very difficult indeed for anyone hoping to learn more about Bruce Lee's life and philosophy. It is equally frustrating for those of us in the martial arts who have longed to learn more about particular aspects of his fighting art.

Fortunately, my friend John Little, whom I've come to know quite well over the past twelve months, has succeeded in this respect. He is to be commended for tackling this monumental task of writing the definitive book on Bruce Lee's philosophy. John has spent over two years and traveled to at least three continents in an effort to gather all of the written and spoken words of Bruce Lee. Intermingling Bruce's material with his own well-researched comments, John has created a comprehensive book with seventeen chapters under three major headings.

One may read this book from beginning to end, or one may choose to read any chapter whose heading seems to be interesting, because each chapter was written on a particular aspect of Bruce's philosophy and, therefore, stands alone. Yet when all the chapters are combined, they form a cohesive body. This book covers many aspects of Bruce's philosophy, his personal views on the issue of relationships (at different levels), and his approach to overcoming adversity and stress. There is even a chapter that John has devoted entirely to the five films Bruce produced, wherein he goes to great lengths to describe the interesting background of each film and the hidden messages that Bruce attempted to convey to its viewers.

Also included are excerpts from a rare personal interview that John conducted with the late Brandon Lee, Bruce's son, that reveals a probing, inquisitive mind very much like his father's. This chapter provides the reader with a rare glimpse of Brandon's life, his personality, and his aspirations in becoming a successful actor.

In the appendixes are two very informative essays by Alan Watts (a philosopher whom Bruce was particularly impressed by) as well as John Little's chronological list of the important events in Bruce's life and a listing of Bruce's principal works. These are valuable records for anyone wishing to know more about Bruce's accomplishments and contributions. For the martial artist at large, this book provides a valuable reference to better understand the philosophical foundations of Bruce Lee's unarmed combative art. For the JKD practitioner, the three stages of cultivation in Bruce Lee's martial art and the four-step guide to self-enlightenment are fully explored.

Since I was born, raised, and educated in China, and have been teaching the Chinese language and culture at Pasadena College for over eleven years as well as serving as a Chinese language translator and lecturer on medical terminology at the SAMRA University of Chinese Traditional Medicine in Los Angeles, I would like to make a comment regarding the English translation of jeet kune do. It has been commonly translated as "the way of the intercepting fist," and this is quite acceptable. I would like to expand the meaning of this translation however. The word *Tao* (pronounced "dao" in

Mandarin and "doe" in Cantonese) means "the way of nature" or "the creative force governing the universe." Thus the term *jeet kune do* written in the Chinese language would mean "the intercepting fist that follows the principles of Tao."

The same word in the Japanese language, *do*, carries the meaning "the way of" or "the method of." Thus, the following Japanese terms are translated as indicated: *judo*, "the way of gentleness"; *kendo*, "the way of sword fighting"; *aikido*, "the way of harmonizing the *chi*"; *shodo*, "the method of calligraphy."

The Chinese sage Lao-tzu, the author of the *Tao te ching*, stated:

Tao *is that from which all things in the universe are created. The process by which all things are created is produced by this energy or* Ch'i, *which originates from* Tao. *This energy is divided into two aspects: Yin and Yang. All things in the universe have Yin energy and Yang energy. When Yin and Yang energies merge together, they produce a state of harmony.*

Bruce was so influenced by this concept of the harmonious existence of the *Yin/Yang* energies that he chose the Yin/Yang symbol (which is referred to by the Chinese as the *T'ai Chi*, the "Grand Ultimate") to be his school emblem in order to represent the core principle of his JKD fighting art, which contains and utilizes both the firm and pliable energies of Yin/Yang.

Bruce added two arrows around the T'ai Chi circle to further emphasize that the JKD fighting techniques must contain the harmonious interplay of Yin (pliable, yielding) and Yang (firm, assertive) energies. He emphasized that in his JKD fighting art, one does not oppose force with force but rather "complements" one's opponent's strong force with Yin, or yielding, energy.

In his writings, Bruce stated metaphorically that "the stiffest tree is easily cracked under pressure, but the bamboo survives by bending with the wind."

He also wrote: "Be like water because it is soft, resilient, and formless. It can never be snapped."

Since Bruce's passing, I have been training continually in JKD in my backyard with a few of my own students. I have closely followed Bruce's teaching. Aside from developing hard-hitting and powerful kicks, I have also trained in t'ai chi ch'uan and push-hand techniques in order to balance my forceful Yang energy with an appropriate degree of Yin energy. I have since studied many Chinese manuscripts on Taoist philosophy and the T'ai Chi Ch'uan classics in order to better understand the nature of Yin/Yang energies and how to develop them.

It is my firm conviction that Bruce believed that JKD training must involve the cultivation of both Yin and Yang energies. The cultivating of Yang energy involves the sharpening of what Bruce called one's martial "tools," or the weapons of offense, such as kicking, punching, and grabbing. One must also raise his quality of execution by improving coordination, precision, speed, and power.

The cultivation of Yin energy, however, involves increasing the sensitivity and pliability of one's body, improving the soft and yielding skill of one's limbs, and cultivating the relaxation of the mind and body, in addition to developing a "detached" attitude of mental poise and emotional calmness. As a result, one is able to move to a higher training level, developing the skill of spontaneous adaptation. This skill allows one to quickly generate the appropriate amount of energy, which complements the opponent's energy almost without conscious effort. During combat, for example, the goal is to use soft and yielding skill (Yin energy) to neutralize the force of one's opponent, rather than attempting to meet your opponent's force (Yang energy) with additional stiff or resisting force (Yang energy).

As soon as one's opponent overextends himself and senses his weakness and retreats (Yin energy), one should attack immediately (Yang energy) to defeat him. This training is very challenging and exciting, and I am far from accomplished at it. As Bruce mentioned in his writings, when one's adaptive skill reaches its highest level, it becomes "as a shadow following effortlessly the moving object," or "as a cork adapting itself to the crests and troughs of the waves."

Bruce also reminded us in his writings that "the height of cultivation should move toward simplicity. It is the halfway cultivation that leads to ornamentation. . . . The process to simplify is like a sculptor who continuously chisels away all the nonessentials until he creates a masterpiece."

The cultivation of the respective Yin and Yang energies are listed in Bruce's book *The Tao of Jeet Kune Do*, which is readily available. I don't know that I will ever reach that level of proficiency in my lifetime, but Bruce will always be my role model and inspiration.

To my fellow JKD practitioners: I hope you will have fun reading this book so that you may truly grasp Bruce's philosophy of JKD. Follow his training program, understand the three stages of cultivation and his four-step guide to self-enlightenment. The information John Little has presented in this book will make your pursuit of JKD a more illuminating and satisfying experience. I would be interested in exchanging ideas and sharing experiences with you (please contact John to get in touch with me).

In closing, then, let me quote from a famous Chinese t'ai chi ch'uan master teacher. When he noticed that his students were learning so many unrelated martial arts while taking his t'ai chi lessons, he admonished them with the following statement:

Many students make the mistake of neglecting that which is near *(that which is readily available and essential to you) to pursue what is* far *(other martial arts that are nonessential or not related to the very art you are learning). Your error in judgment and pursuit will take you thousands of miles off course. Therefore, you must be careful to make a clear distinction between what is essential to you and what is not.*

Daniel Lee
Pasadena, California

The course of a bird in flight pays no attention to the lines of East and West.

—CALLIGRAPHIC INSCRIPTION BY ALAN WATTS

Some time ago, I received a telephone call from Japan from a sincere gentleman who asked if I could recommend a few tapes on Zen by my father. He went on to explain that he had traveled from Seattle to Kyoto to study in a Buddhist monastery but that after several years he still had not received instruction in Zen. He was anxious to learn and was grateful when I directed him to a few favorite recordings.

East meets West: Bruce Lee was a pioneer in using the medium of film to teach Western audiences—and even Western actors, such as John Saxon (left)— about Eastern philosophy.

Although ironic, this was not surprising, for Zen is not apt to be quickly taught to Westerners in Japan since it is often misunderstood.

It was surprising, however, when recently I discovered that Bruce Lee used to regularly record Alan Watts from the radio or television and play the tapes for his students. In reading his notes and interviews, it is apparent that my father's works were an important influence in his life, and like my father, awareness of the *Tao* was central to his art.

Of course, the phenomenon of an accomplished Easterner teaching his Western students "physical" martial arts while finding "spiritual" inspiration in the works of a Westerner with a lifelong curiosity about Eastern wisdom is certainly unusual. But as John Little notes, "the problem with the Western approach is that it attempts to *explain* life as opposed to revealing how to *experience* it."

Both Lee and Watts were involved in teaching endeavors that were in a sense attempts to "speak the unspeakable," to communicate the essence of something that can be understood only directly. In Taoism, they found a uniquely practical philosophy dedicated to, as it were, revealing the purposelessness of life. For in directing ourselves toward a goal, we invariably point our attention ahead and outside of the present moment, and as my father was fond of saying, "If the goal of dancing were to reach a certain spot on the floor, then obviously the fastest dancer would be the best. The point of dancing is the dance itself." And so it is with life.

The historical division between the "objectionably objective" Western world and the richly subjective East has, in the twentieth century, begun to close, so that today the characteristic ways of experiencing the world attributed to each are seen in direct contrast all over the world. And although the significance of the symbolism on a colorful Yin/Yang T-shirt worn by an American youngster is probably not well understood, the extended arm from the car in front of me in traffic gracefully performing the movements of t'ai chi ch'uan is obviously connected to an inwardly centered being, who at least experientially understands something of the philosophy that inspired both Alan Watts and Bruce Lee. For in the words of Bruce Lee:

Life lives, and in the living flow—no questions are raised. The reason is that life is a living NOW! Completeness, the now, is an absence of the con-

scious mind to strive to divide that which is indivisible. For once the completeness of things is taken apart, it is no longer complete.

In these words, Bruce Lee revealed that he had discovered a secret that seems to elude most modern people. The secret, simply put, is that although we can simultaneously live and contemplate life, to do so takes something out of it, for the reflective aspect of the self is not the whole—or complete—self. As David Bohm, the British physicist, said, "The trouble with the small self is that it thinks it's the big self."

On the following pages, one will find essential ideas once expressed by Alan Watts, Krishnamurti, both Suzukis, Joseph Campbell, and many others—and long before by Lao-tzu, Chuang-tzu, Buddha, and Shankara. Although many of these ideas are not new, their expression embodies a living art that points to a way of liberation my father once described as the "religion of no religion."

Finally, it appears that after Eastern and Western cultures passed while heading in opposite directions, the stage is now set for the development of an East/West culture based upon the best of each—the adventurous spirit and curiosity of the West and the highly developed philosophical and aesthetic sensibilities of the East. The mutual receptivity of these elements has already contributed greatly to the birth of well-integrated ways of knowing. It now only remains to be seen if the directions of each culture will come around in a full circle to dance together in the classic image of T'ai Chi.

Mark Watts
San Anselmo, California

hile it may come as a profound surprise to those of us who are in the throes of an emotional or life crisis, the fact remains that the answer to virtually all of our problems resides within us already. It exists in the form of a vast reservoir of free-flowing energy that, when channeled to our muscles, can give us great strength and, when channeled to our brain, can give us great insight and understanding. The Chinese call this naturally occurring energy "chi," and it is their belief that it circulates in continuous cycles within our bodies.

Some have compared this vast inner energy to the quantum theory in physics; that is, the subatomic energy patterns that are held to be synonymous with the evolutionary forces underlying the growth and development

Bruce Lee was able to generate tremendous inner power, or what is referred to in Chinese as chi.

of all things. This energy is not observable in, say, the way in which particles or other solid forms of matter are, and yet it is not exactly a wave or a
process, either. Evidently it is more a combination of the two. In any event,
as we shall soon learn, all of life apes this energy cycle in processes that are
readily discernible—from the atom to the solar system. The dividend in our
learning to tap into these vast energy cycles is that doing so can result in a
complete and total harmony of mind and body that reaches its culmination
in the form of a great spiritual awakening, what the Taoist sages of ancient
China called *tun-wu*, and the Japanese Zen masters call *satori*.

The legendary twentieth-century martial artist Bruce Lee, not surprisingly, was fully cognizant of the existence of these great forces, causing
him to once comment:

> *I feel I have this great creative and spiritual force within me that is greater
> than faith, greater than ambition, greater than confidence, greater than
> determination, greater than vision. It is all these combined. . . . Whether
> it is the godhead or not, I feel this great force, this untapped power, this
> dynamic something within me. This feeling defies description, and there is
> no experience with which this feeling may be compared. It is something like
> a strong emotion mixed with faith, but a lot stronger.*

If I might be so bold as to attempt to symbolize this great inner energy
force, perhaps it would best be represented by the image of a martial artist
or *warrior*. After all, the warrior is an image symbolizing one aspect of a great
force that, if marshaled properly, can win many battles for you but, if mis-
directed or neglected, can rise up to become your nemesis. Most of us in the
West have neglected our warrior force, ignoring its presence and forgoing
even the attempt to connect with it. The end result is that we end up
becoming far less than we are fully capable of. As American psychologist
William James once noted in his essay entitled "The Energies of Men":
"Compared with what we ought to be, we are only half awake. Our fires
are damped, our drafts are checked. We are making use of only a small part
of our possible mental and physical resources."[1]

If, however, we choose instead to tap into this inner energy, we become
all that we ultimately can be—instantly awakening our passions and fanning
fully the flames of our ultimate potential—and our lives change. We become

more passionate, more certain—more at ease with ourselves and the world around us—and we succeed, almost effortlessly, at our objectives. Certainly Bruce Lee was able to tap into his warrior force at will, and it was his belief that great things were possible when we learned to channel what he termed *"those great spiritual forces within"* with an eye toward the future: *"When man comes to a conscious vital realization of those great spiritual forces within himself and begins to use those forces in science, in business, and in life, his progress in the future will be unparalleled."*

NBA superstar Kareem Abdul-Jabbar, who studied privately with Bruce Lee for a period of six years, recalled how Lee taught him how to tap into his own warrior within:

> *Bruce showed me how to harness some of what was raging inside me and summon it completely at my will. The Chinese call it* chi; *the Japanese,* ki; *the Indians,* prana—*it is the life force, and it is incredibly powerful. . . . It sounds bizarre, and it can't be explained adequately except to those who have already experienced it, but it's one of the very few willable miracles.*[2]

To say that this creative power, when channeled correctly, has the potential to be successful is an understatement. After all, when Lee applied it to the realm of business (after appearing in only two films), he negotiated with the company that produced his films and caused them to create a brand-new production company—of which he was a 50 percent shareholder. When he applied it to love, both he and his wife (who also applied his philosophic principles to their relationship) were able to overcome racial differences, cultural mores, and the bigoted opinions of those who would oppose their love. Bruce Lee also utilized this creative force in developing the revolutionary principles underlying his martial art of jeet kune do.

The cultivation of the warrior within has as its first requisite the comprehension of a philosophical perspective that, to many of us in the West, will surely represent a brand-new outlook on life and on the ways of the world. This book is an attempt to present just such a perspective through the philosophical insights left to us by Bruce Lee. It has long been my contention that what set Lee apart from every other martial artist of his generation was not his physical prowess (as remarkable as this was) but his mind, and that his insights and philosophical perceptions have a much broader application than may have heretofore been considered.

My contribution then, if you'd care to call it that, is not to the substance of Lee's philosophy, which is entirely his achievement, but to the form of its presentation. My intention within these pages to take both the message and teachings of Bruce Lee and present them in a manner that will, hopefully, have some relevance to your life, whatever your occupation.

ACKNOWLEDGMENTS

My appreciation in preparing this book extends to many people. First and foremost, immeasurable thanks is owed to the man whose perspective and philosophy of life I'm presenting within these pages, Bruce Lee. Lee's words and example first served to open this writer's eyes to the pleasures of philosophy and ultimately brought about the awakening of my own inner warrior. Further thanks are extended to those individuals and thinkers from whom Lee learned a great deal, either directly, from people such as his first (and only) martial arts instructor, Yip Man, or indirectly, through the writings of philosophers of the first order such as Lao-tzu, Confucius, Alan Watts, Jiddu Krishnamurti, and Daisetz T. Suzuki.

Appreciation is also extended to Linda Lee Cadwell, Lee's widow, whose insight into his philosophy as well as the viewpoints she shared concerning additional philosophical influences served to broaden my understanding of her late husband's belief system. In addition, I would like to acknowledge the support and example set by Adrian Marshall, who was Bruce Lee's lawyer from 1969 until Lee's passing in 1973. Both Linda and Adrian have given me solid encouragement in my pursuit to present and preserve what I take to be the true legacy of Bruce Lee. Above this, however, they have also entrusted me with their friendship. I also want to thank Bruce Lee's students, particularly Ted Wong, Daniel Lee, Taky Kimura, and Dan Inosanto, who shared with me some of Lee's philosophic materials that he gave out to students of his Chinatown school in the late 1960s, and with whom I have spent countless hours discussing his ideas in general and his philosophy in particular.

Most of all I want to thank the late Brandon Lee, whose conversation with me in August 1992 caused me to seriously examine the significance of the spiritual side of the martial arts and to dedicate myself wholeheartedly to the task of locating and disseminating authentic firsthand materials that expounded his father's unique philosophy and incredible legacy.

Many of the publications from which I've excerpted materials are now defunct. Other statements made by Bruce Lee that have been excerpted are either from his personal notes and essays or from Little-Wolff Creative Group's extensive selection. In all cases, however, an attempt was made to locate either the authors or publishers of these materials for permissions. To the men and women who wrote, recorded, and videotaped their dialogues with Bruce Lee, I owe a huge debt of gratitude for their work in preserving this man's unique philosophy. To this end, I would like to thank the following publishers and journals for the selections that have been excerpted in this work: *Seattle Times*, *Seattle Post-Intelligencer*, *Springfield Union News*, Ted Thomas, Alex Ben Block, *Hong Kong Standard*, *Gastonia Gazette*, Pierre Berton/Elsa Franklin, *Miami News* ("Florida Report"), *Movie Mirror*, *TV and Movie Screen*, *TV/Radio Mirror*, and Little-Wolff Creative Group.

I particularly want to thank Ohara Publications and *Black Belt* magazine for their invaluable assistance and permission to quote from their extensive catalog of authentic Bruce Lee materials and for the tremendous ongoing work they've done in perpetuating the art and philosophy of Bruce Lee.

EPIGRAMMATIC INSIGHTS FROM THE PHILOSOPHY OF BRUCE LEE

Life is a constant process of relating.

∞

Man, the living creature, the creating individual, is always more important than any established style.

∞

Gung fu is not preoccupied with breaking bricks and smashing boards. . . . We're more concerned with having it affect our whole way of thinking and behaving.

∞

Brandon is being brought up in the midst of two cultures. There are good points in Chinese culture; there are good points in Occidental culture. He will be taught to take some principles from one, some from the other. Brandon will learn that Oriental culture and Occidental culture are not mutually exclusive, but mutually dependent. Neither would be remarkable if it were not for the existence of the other.

Linda and I aren't one and one. We are two halves that make a whole. You have to apply yourself to be a family—two halves fitted together are more efficient than either half would ever be alone!

∞

It sounded at first like typical houseboy stuff. I told Dozier, "Look, if you sign me up with all that pigtail and hopping around jazz, forget it." In the past, the typical casting has been that kind of stereotype. Like with the Indians. You never see a human being Indian on television.

∞

The main thing is teaching a man to do his thing, just be himself. . . . I'm against trying to impose a style on a man. This is an art, an expression of a man's own self.

∞

You can't organize truth. That's like trying to put a pound of water into wrapping paper and shaping it.

∞

Because of styles, people are separated. They are not united together because styles became law, man. The original founder of the style started out with hypothesis. But now it has become the gospel truth, and people who go into it become the product of it. It doesn't matter how you are, who you are, how you are structured, how you are built, or how you are made . . . it doesn't seem to matter. You just go in there and become that product. And that, to me, is not right.

Whenever he had a spare moment or two (which wasn't often), Lee would busy himself in crafting aphoristic statements that conveyed profound truths.

The greatest help is self-help; there is no other help but self-help—doing one's best, dedicating oneself wholeheartedly to a given task, which happens to have no end but is an ongoing process.

∽

All the time people come up and say, "Bruce—are you really that good?" I say, "Well, if I tell you I'm good, probably you'll say I'm boasting. But if I tell you I'm no good, you'll know I'm lying."

∽

All types of knowledge ultimately mean self-knowledge.

Empty your mind. Be formless. Shapeless. Like water. Now you put water into a cup, it becomes the cup. You put water into a bottle, it becomes the bottle. You put it in a teapot, it becomes the teapot. Now water can flow, or it can crash. Be water, my friend.

∞

I believe that I have a role here in Southeast Asia. The audience needs to be educated, and the one to educate them has to be somebody who is responsible. We are dealing with the masses, and we have to create something that will get through to them. We have to educate them step by step. We can't do it overnight. That's what I am doing right now. Whether I succeed or not remains to be seen. But I don't just feel committed, I am committed.

∞

Through the ages, the end of heroes is the same as ordinary men. They all died and gradually faded away in the memory of man. But when we are still alive, we have to understand ourselves, discover ourselves, and express ourselves.

∞

Knowing is not enough; we must apply. Willing is not enough; we must do.

∞

I don't want to sound like "As Confucius say," but under the sky, under the heavens, there is but one family. It just so happens that people are different.

SOME THOUGHTS ABOUT BRUCE LEE

He was very proud of being Chinese, and he wanted to show the rest of the world part of the Chinese culture through films. Not just the fighting— he wanted to add in a little bit of philosophy. He studied all the traditional philosophies, but then he began to form his own philosophy, and he came to the realization that you just can't borrow another person's philosophy. You have to learn about yourself and create your own philosophy, your own way of life. Bruce believed that the most important thing in the world is the individual and that each individual must have knowledge of himself before he can relate to other people. He managed to cross the barriers in communication with people.

LINDA LEE

There's something about a man who makes you believe in yourself. It's a very special power that only a master has. Bruce made you excel by making you believe in the impossible. Under his tutelage everything was possible. All doubts were cast aside.

STIRLING SILLIPHANT
(STUDENT OF BRUCE LEE)

Bruce had great inner strength, or chi. You locate the core of your body—two inches below your navel—and it's a sort of a realization that everything comes from there. Sort of like the axis of the wheel of your car, where even a short turn of the axle can rotate the entire circumference of the wheel. It's like an adrenaline flow that you can tap into in emergency situations. He could just call forth that energy at will.

TAKY KIMURA
(STUDENT OF BRUCE LEE)

Bruce taught many Japanese and American students. But, being Chinese, I was able to absorb his philosophy perhaps a little more easily than most. He talked about T'ai Chi, Yin-Yang, hardness and softness, the philosophy of Lao-tzu, and so on. He was an ardent student of all sorts of philosophy and was very much interested in Lao-tzu and believed in the phrase "Using no way as way, having no limitation as limitation." I would always marvel after every lesson I had with Bruce because each lesson was like a philosophy in action. He wasn't just talking about "punch this" or "punch that" on a mechanical or physical level. He was always talking about the philosophical part that underlined it. For instance, the Yin-Yang, or the "water principle": he would place that principle clearly in your mind and then implement that principle into your action. This was a different approach to martial-arts instruction. We studied philosophy with Bruce because he had philosophy as his underlying theme and direction. He was really my mentor in showing the linkage between philosophy and martial art. They're inseparable.

DANIEL LEE
(STUDENT OF BRUCE LEE)

He was very worldly. He could pick any subject and talk intelligently about it. And not just martial arts; he majored in philosophy, and a lot of times I would go to him for advice and ask him lots of questions. He would always take time to hear me out and then help me to think about things in an entirely new way. He really gave me some good advice—not just in martial art but in life in general.

TED WONG
(STUDENT OF BRUCE LEE)

He felt very strongly that if he could get people to appreciate something in the Chinese culture, then they would appreciate something in other cultures as well. He felt that he was doing his small part in establishing something toward world peace and harmony and understanding among other people of different cultures.

DANIEL INOSANTO
(STUDENT OF BRUCE LEE)

He was a teacher first of all. He taught philosophy and tried to spread knowledge and wisdom. That's why he took on the martial-arts establishment the way he did. Because a lot of what they were talking about was hypocrisy and really just something that gave them the ability to scam people who wanted to learn martial arts. The integrity with which Bruce lived his life and tried to uphold what he believed to be right—that is a clear example of how it ought to be done. No matter what it is you're doing, do it with total honesty and total dedication. He definitely influenced me.

KAREEM ABDUL-JABBAR
(STUDENT OF BRUCE LEE)

Farewell, my brother. It has been an honor to share this space and time with you. As a friend and as a teacher, you have given to me and have brought my physical, spiritual, and psychological selves together. Thank you. May peace be with you.

JAMES COBURN
(STUDENT OF BRUCE LEE)

To some people, I'm sure he's just that guy who does those chop-socky movies on Saturday morning, you know? Whereas to someone else he has influenced and changed their lives because of his amazing philosophies that he wrote about. To somebody else he's the most amazing martial artist, and it continues to surprise me that he's so well known around the world. I think he did a lot for the Asian community in Hollywood. I think he was a real pioneer in many different fields.

SHANNON LEE

He was my father. He raised me. I guess the martial arts, which are an integral part of my life, come entirely from my father. . . . I mean, he started me in the martial arts when I could walk. He trained me my entire life until he passed away, and then, even when I continued my training, it was with one of his students. So while I've had some different influences throughout the course of my martial arts training, essentially the martial arts to me is so connected to my dad that it's almost like they're not different at all. I guess that's the strongest influence.

BRANDON LEE

I cannot teach you, only help you to explore yourself. Nothing more.

BRUCE LEE

Part One

SEEING THE TOTALITY

CHAPTER ONE

THE TRUE MEANING OF GUNG FU

Gung fu is a philosophy; it's an integral part of the philosophies of Tao-
ism and Buddhism, the ideals of giving with adversity, to bend slightly and
then spring up stronger than before, to have patience in all things, to profit
by one's mistakes and lessons in life. These are the many-sided aspects of
the art of gung fu; it teaches the way to live, as well as the way to protect
oneself.

BRUCE LEE

Ron was out on the seventeenth fairway having another great day. All afternoon he'd broken par on every hole, and the seventeenth would prove to be no exception. His golfing partner that day was a Chinese gentleman by the name of Li Tsung. After Ron completed the eighteenth hole—and another birdie—Li Tsung slapped his partner on the back. "Ron," he said with a smile, "you're a man of gung fu."

"*Gung fu?*" answered Ron with a bemused look on his face. "I don't know anything about flying through the air and kicking people in the teeth!" He chuckled at his retort and then continued: "I'm a golfer, Li—a *golfer*. You should learn to pronounce the word as, judging by today's performance, I'd say I was a pretty *accomplished* one!"

"I didn't say you were efficient at flying kicks," explained Li Tsung. "I said you were a man of gung fu—and your last statement simply underscores this fact."

Lee recounts the story "The Three Japanese Swordsmen" during an appearance on Hong Kong television in 1970.

"You've lost me," said Ron, placing his putter back in his golf bag. "Isn't gung fu, or whatever you call it, what that Bruce Lee guy did?"

"Indeed," replied Li Tsung. "And it's also what you've displayed out here on the links today."

This story illustrates a common difference between Eastern and Western perception of the martial arts. Li Tsung was quite correct in his interpretation of the term *gung fu*, and this is not altogether unexpected from a man well-versed in Eastern culture. Equally as predictable is Ron's interpretation of gung fu as being simply a form of combat. You see, we in the West have been guilty of bastardizing the true meaning of the term *kung fu*, or *gung fu* as Bruce Lee, being Cantonese, preferred to pronounce it. To people in the West, the term is now synonymous with Asian combative methods, interpreted as a fighting skill like "karate" or "tae kwon do." This, however, is not at all in keeping with the original Chinese meaning of the term.

Gung fu, according to the authentic Chinese translation, is a term used to denote a tremendous sense of *total* achievement or accomplishment. A master of gung fu, then, is one who displays tremendous proficiency in one's craft, and this craft could, in effect, be anything. A journalist, for example, who is an exceptionally good writer can be said to have gung fu. A painter who possesses exceptional skill can likewise be said to display gung fu—and so on, with all professions and pastimes, from medicine to horseback riding and from—you guessed it—martial arts to golf.

By today's standards, gung fu is revealed through a thorough mastery of one's job, and through this achievement, a mastery of oneself is also revealed. Self-mastery—at least from the Chinese perspective—is a very positive and desirable thing for an individual to strive for. According to venerated Chinese tradition, a gung fu master revealed his mastery of self by being a considerable philosopher, a talented alchemist, a well-versed medical practitioner, a well-read student of prose and literature, as well as a musician of some note. Oh, yes, a gung fu master would also be quite able to defend himself or his loved ones should the need arise. However, as you can see, to use the term *gung fu* simply as a synonym for fighting ability is to do the term a gross injustice.

A Tale of Three Swordsmen

Bruce Lee, the man considered by many to be the embodiment of the term *gung fu* in its original and purest sense, was fond of relating the tale called "The Three Japanese Swordsmen" whenever discussing gung fu. This fable involving the famed Japanese *kensai* (sword-saint) Miyamoto Musashi so impressed Lee with its subtle symbolism that he recounted it for a national television audience in Hong Kong and even wrote it into his introduction for a screenplay entitled *The Silent Flute* that he had created along with actor James Coburn and writer Stirling Silliphant. The tale, as Lee related it, goes as follows:

> *Three swordsmen sat down at a table in a crowded Japanese inn and began to make loud comments about their neighbor, hoping to goad him into a duel. The master [Musashi, the greatest samurai in all Japan] seemed to take no notice of them, but when their remarks became ruder and more pointed, he raised his chopsticks and, in quick snips, effortlessly caught four flies on the wing. As he slowly laid down the chopsticks, the three swordsmen hurriedly left the room.*

The reason that the swordsmen suddenly lost interest in harassing Musashi wasn't the fact, as some of us in the West might hastily surmise, that they were intrigued by this man's ability to catch flies with chopsticks. Instead, they recognized that the skill this man revealed through his actions with the chopsticks was an indicator of supreme gung fu—of complete mastery over himself—and therefore, he was a man to be avoided. Their conclusion underscores the age-old Chinese belief that any person who attains complete mastery of any art reveals his presence of mind in every action.

The ancient gung fu masters were said to be skillful masseurs, herbalists, and acupuncturists. Western medicine has only recently begun to accept or even acknowledge these treatments for maladies of the body, mind, and spirit. For example, it was only when it was revealed that an herb like *ma huang*, a 1,000-year-old Chinese cure for asthma, actually contained ephedrine—the same thing that doctors in the West prescribe for the condition—that Western medicine realized that they might have reached their verdict on at least some of ways of the East in haste. Similarly, the ancient art of acupuncture, now a common treatment in Western sports medicine clinics for its miraculous healing and anesthetic powers, came into gung fu training years ago but was rejected for the better part of the twentieth century by Western medicine.

There is a strong impulse in the Western mind to instantly identify or compartmentalize everything we encounter by placing things into convenient categories. Typically these categories come down to just two subheadings, Safe and Unsafe. Those things with which we are, to a certain degree, familiar are placed under the former heading, and the different, unknown, or foreign are instantly placed under the latter.

The end result of such a practice is that we often find ourselves far too busy labeling and standing outside of life to actually take part in it or, at least, to enjoy it to any great degree. In short, we lack the grander perspective that is gung fu. According to Bruce Lee:

> *Gung fu is practiced not only for health and self-protection but for cultivation of the mind as well. Gung fu was used by Taoist priests and Chinese monks as a philosophy, or way of thinking, in which the ideals of giving*

with adversity, to bend slightly and then spring up stronger than before, are practiced. The qualities of patience and profiting from one's mistakes are a part of the discipline of gung fu.

It will, then, perhaps come as a shock to some people that Bruce Lee, a man known in the West primarily as a star of action films and as a fighter par excellence, was indeed a man of gung fu as the term was originally used. Lee was a philosopher, a man concerned with issues of human conduct and a man who strove to understand the vast and complex world around him, and it can be said in retrospect that Lee was a *successful* philosopher. In fact, given the accuracy of his words and truly global following his films and words have attained, it can be said with some degree of accuracy that the man was a *sage*.

Lee's words contain wisdom that belied his years and that reveal an understanding of considerable depth. This is not to imply that his perceptions on the human condition simply came to him intuitively. Lee studied long and hard varied books on philosophy, religion, and spirituality. He read and reread passages by men such as Lao-tzu, Chuang-tzu, Sun-tzu, Confucius, Tzu Yeh, Socrates, Plato, Baruch Spinoza, René Descartes, and David Hume, as well as the more modern sages such as Jiddu Krishnamurti, D. T. Suzuki, and Alan Watts. He searched among their words for eternal verities and attempted to learn more about the ultimate nature of the soul, the universe out of which it grew, and of humankind in general. It was philosophy that was truly Lee's passion. The martial arts were simply the route he chose to express it.

Fortunately, Lee was not loath to share his beliefs with others. In fact, it was through his public interviews that his message and beliefs were, perhaps, delivered most eloquently. Some of the reporters to whom he spoke recognized his brilliance and saved their audiotapes or videos for the purpose of personal edification and review. Most did not. Still, those of us today who wish to learn from this inspired thinker are fortunate that the audio- and videotaped fragments of Lee's public discussions that have survived and the written words that he left behind have preserved a philosophical perspective that is unmatched for understanding, enjoying, and living life to its fullest possible measure.

The Ultimate Evolution of Martial Art

Like the true meaning of gung fu, Bruce Lee's philosophy encompasses far more than mere technical fighting skill. Indeed, to fully appreciate the man's philosophy, one has to look beyond the physical confines of the martial arts. After all, we are now knocking on the door of the twenty-first century, and mankind's skill in martial art has evolved to the point of the Stealth bomber and the Uzi machine gun. While spending many hours a week in intensive, elaborate, and often highly technical training in the arts of hand-to-hand combat is laudable, in terms of developing diligence and cultivating a proficiency in such techniques, it is nevertheless true that one's chances of successfully employing such skills in an encounter on today's streets remain at best remote, particularly in a world where weapons reign supreme.

The amount of practice required, for example, to develop proficiency in the manipulation of ancient Okinawan flailing implements (which were originally incorporated into ancient fighting arts for the express purpose of knocking Japanese horsemen from their mounts), seems now, for the most part, to be a rather outmoded and impractical way to prepare for the possibility of an attack on today's streets. In fact, a glance at our daily newspapers would tend to indicate that most assailants in this day and age don't share the martial artist's love for nostalgia. As a result, more martial artists have been killed on the streets of New York than were taken down at the height of China's Boxer Rebellion—and, ironically, for exactly the same reason: the inherent inability of the philosophies of most martial artists to keep pace with the combative evolution of the times.

Statistics now indicate that within our major cities, people carry weapons that can end your life from thirty to ninety feet away and sometimes from an even greater distance. This being the case, to devote the better part of one's life to learning the fighting skills that were originally developed to overcome the empty-handed adversary of the past in order to defend yourself against the automatic-weapon-carrying assailant of the present doesn't make a lot of sense. The rules have changed. The world is different. And martial artists, for the most part, need to get their clocks fixed.

This is not to indicate that martial arts training has nothing to offer us in this day and age; it's just that concentrating solely on the combative element of it is unnecessary if your objective is to search for truth and to lead a more rewarding life. The enduring value in studying a martial art lies in its serving as a vehicle through which to express yourself and, through such expression, to come to understand yourself better, spiritually speaking, through a progressively evolving knowledge of both your limitations and capabilities.

I can hear the protests already. "But certainly the martial arts are still effective in certain types of self-defense situations!" Indeed, they are—but then, so is the tomahawk. However, neither are up to the task of defending you against a spray of bullets from the barrel of a semiautomatic weapon like those used in the drive-by shootings so common in the streets of our major cities these days. Again, the martial arts are useful; they serve as wonderful precursors to health and spiritual cultivation, but the notion of incorporating any of these arts as a legitimate means of self-defense against the weapons found on today's streets is impractical at best and, at worst, a foolish and downright deadly mistake. Bruce Lee himself realized this fact of combative evolution and said as much in the famous video *The Lost Interview*: *"Nowadays you don't go around on the street punching people or kicking people, because if you do, somebody will just pull out a gun and—Pow! That's it. I mean, I don't care how good you are in martial arts."*

Bruce Lee, as you will soon learn, was very *real-world* oriented and, therefore, very much against wasting time preparing for improbable encounters. While he admired the beauty and skill necessary to achieve proficiency in the various arts, he realized that for the most part, they were dinosaur drills. Even as far back as the early 1960s, Lee realized that the training habits of most martial artists were like organized dance classes; people were taught movements that looked beautiful and impressive, but if you ever attempted to employ them to defend yourself or your loved ones on the street, your chances of survival would be about the same as the student of the dance class.

Lee even had devised a mock tombstone that sat upon his office desk and revealed to visitors his attitude toward those who blindly followed the classical traditions of the past instead of evolving with the martial advancements of the present. The inscription read:

IN MEMORY OF A ONCE FLUID MAN
CRAMMED AND DISTORTED BY THE CLASSICAL MESS.

During an audio interview conducted by journalist Alex Ben Block, Lee put it even more succinctly:

Most martial arts instructors are so doggone stubborn, you know? I mean their attitude is "Well, two hundred years ago it was taught like this, therefore it should be continued to be taught like this." To maintain that type of attitude—I mean, you've had it! You will still be back in [that time capsule]. You will never grow, because learning is a discovering thing. It's a constant process of discovery. Whereas, if we follow the old method, it is simply a continuous repetition of what was being handed down several hundred years ago.

Lee labeled the repetition of such outdated martial arts practices "organized despair," and he sought throughout the remainder of his life for a more twentieth-century approach to the age-old problem of combating adversity— in all of its forms.

For this reason, Bruce Lee's true legacy extends far beyond the simple confines of the martial arts world. His philosophy no more belongs exclusively to martial artists than Nietzsche's belonged exclusively to Hitler and Nazi Germany. Lee was an artist, a humanitarian, and above all else, a thinker. He was a man whose eloquence—as opposed to his fists—swayed politicians, executives, movie stars, and people of a less lofty social status alike. More important, Lee was a man whose thoughts and philosophy enabled him to cope successfully with racism, financial difficulty, love, pain, joy, sadness, wonder, marriage, fatherhood, and friendship—with life, in other words.

While Lee's teachings within the field of martial arts are limited to what a human being might accomplish with his four limbs, his teachings within the field of the mind remain infinite.

It is in this spirit of personal evolution through the discovery and ultimate mastery of oneself that we shall now proceed. If this concept sounds to you a little like the true meaning of the term *gung fu*, you're starting to get the picture.

The second gadget I have in mind is used to dramatize the not too alive way of the classical so called Kung Fu styles. [miniature] What I have in mind is a "tomb stone" and here is the drawing

IN MEMORY OF A ONCE FLUID MAN CRAMMED AND DISTORTED BY THE CLASSICAL MESS

I'm sure you know how a grave looks like and make it with any material you like (aluminum tomb stone is fine) and at any size you want. Not too small though, because it's for display.

Call me collect if you have any problem. Thank you in anticipation   Bruce

In a page written to his friend and student George Lee (no relation) in the mid-1960s, Bruce Lee outlined the design and message he wanted placed on a miniature tombstone that, in his words, "expresses my feelings perfectly" (regarding the traditional forms of martial art).

CHAPTER TWO

EMPTYING OUR CUP

*I*f Bruce Lee's philosophy is to have any enduring meaning to the great majority of us who are not practicing martial artists, we shall have to look to the higher principles that form the root of his belief system. Once these have been established, we can then apply them to a broader base of problems that we'll be more likely to encounter during the course of our day-to-day existence. After all, not all of us will be asked to step outside and get into a hand-to-hand street fight on our way home from work tonight or, for that matter, at the golf course this weekend. All of us do, however, need to know more about ourselves and the world around us in order to better learn how to deal with the many adversities that life always seems to throw at us. To this end, we need to understand our lives as they fit into the universe as a whole.

The Tao

It doesn't matter if you prefer the way of the West or the way of the East; underpinning both of these is *the way of the universe*, the common denominator that interconnects the greater totality. To comprehend this, independent of whatever our personal prejudices might happen to be for the moment, is to experience freedom at both its highest and lowest levels—in toto, in other words. The Chinese call this metaphysical "lay of the land" *Tao*, and it may be appropriate to comment on it briefly at this juncture.

If the universe can be compared to a vast ocean, we—as human beings—can be likened to the individual waves that come into and pass out of existence on its surface. Each of the waves are distinct from the others and yet still interconnected to the ocean itself. This entire oceanic process—whatever its form (i.e., flowing, ebbing, dripping, waving, vortexing, etc.)—would be Tao. (Please see Alan Watts' comments on this in the essay "Eco-Zen" in the appendix at the end of this book.)

According to Bruce Lee, Tao can only be comprehended by a mind that is free from distraction:

> The principle of gung fu is not a thing that can be learned, like a science, by fact-finding and instruction in facts. It has to grow spontaneously, like a flower, in a mind free from emotions and desires. The core of this principle of gung fu is "Tao"—the spontaneity of the universe. The word Tao has no exact equivalent in the English language. . . . I have used the word Truth for it—the Truth behind gung fu, the Truth that every gung fu practitioner should follow.

Some of you reading this might be saying: "Wait a minute, this boat's heading into uncharted waters here. This talk of universal realities and Tao is foreign to me—I'm not at all comfortable with it. In fact, I don't comprehend how knowing *the way of the universe* is going to help me solve *my* problems!" But that's where you're wrong, dear reader. To know your problem—that is, to be able to recognize a *true* problem (which is something you have a say in altering)—is very important, but few people ever learn to identify a true problem throughout the course of their lifetime. That you experience problems is a fact. That you need to is another matter entirely.

Unfortunately, if you look to Western philosophic method for a solution to these problems, you find that it typically creates more problems than it solves. For example, near the end of his magnum opus, *Tractatus Logico-Philosophicus*, the philosopher Ludwig Wittgenstein (1889–1951) revealed that what we typically consider to be "major" philosophical problems are meaningless questions and that "solving" them consists not of answers, but of understanding their inherent meaninglessness. Once this fact is realized, once it's understood that "the meaning of life" is that it has no meaning at all, relief from these "problems" is simultaneous. In fact, all that we can be certain of are the observable facts of existence. As Wittgenstein states in the first of the seven propositions contained within the *Tractatus*: "The world is all that is the case."

While there is indeed some merit to these propositions, Wittgenstein went on to produce a sequence of numbered observations about each proposition, or rather observations about the observations about the observations. For instance, the first page of his *Tractatus* begins thus:

1.   The world is all that is the case.

1.1   The world is the totality of facts, not of things.

1.11   The world is determined by the facts, and by their being all the facts.

1.12   For the totality of facts determines what is the case, and also whatever is not the case.

1.13   The facts in logical space are the world.

1.2   The world divides into facts.

1.21   Each item can be the case or not the case while everything else remains the same.

2.   What is the case—a fact—is the existence of states of affairs.[1]

The end result of such hyperanalysis only served to further muddy the very waters Wittgenstein had hoped to clarify. Still, despite Western philosophy's occasional attempts to settle our worries and concerns intellectually (and as we shall learn, a method such as Wittgenstein's—with its emphasis on analysis, analysis, and more analysis—is a step in the wrong direction), we remain a culture that is beset with worries.

Ironically, many of the things that people worry about or consider to be major problems are simply the result of viewing life through the filter of an invalid belief system. This is precisely why it is necessary—crucial, in fact— to come to accurately understand the ways of the universe in which you function. If you first learn *the ways of the universe*, if you first learn exactly what things are in fact actually open to your volitional control (and therefore worthy of your thoughts and concerns) and which ones are not, your life suddenly becomes far less problematic.

If one's personal problems can be likened to the various leaves on the branch of a tree, then their solution lies in one's learning to understand the true nature of the branch that nourishes them and upon which they reside—

or looking deeper still, seeking to understand the very root of the tree that grows the branch containing such problematic leaves. To Lee's way of thinking this was synonymous with Tao, or the universal order of things: *"It is futile to argue as to which single leaf, which design of branches, or which attractive flower you like; when you understand the root, you understand all of its blossoming."*

By way of illustration, allow me to digress a moment. I worked for a time for bodybuilding magnate Joe Weider. Weider had brought me on staff to write articles on subjects pertaining to health and fitness, and as my work included writing reports on bodybuilding contests, air travel was often required. On many such occasions, I found myself on a long flight to some distant locale, made all the longer by the fact that Weider's travel agent had seated me next to a fellow staff member—whom I shall refer to as Jeff—who would not close his mouth from the time he stepped on the plane until the moment we deplaned. Not only would I get to hear every one of Jeff's unsolicited opinions on every aspect of competitive bodybuilding, training, and diet, but his life story as well—starting from DNA to present day.

One day I heard Jeff involved in a heated discussion with another journalist. The journalist with whom he spoke was a knowledgeable individual in his own right, but as he listened patiently for an opportunity to present his perspective on the topic Jeff was holding forth on, Jeff abruptly ended the conversation by stating: "There's no point in your arguing with me about this. I've thought about it much more than you have." With that he turned on his heel, leaving his supposed partner in the conversation completely nonplussed.

While there was no denying that Jeff was indeed quite knowledgeable about the subject matter, the problem was that his need to prove a particular point of view correct had superseded his desire to seek truth. In other words, he had effectively shut himself off from experiencing anything new or different about the subject. Granted, not all of us enjoy a spirited dispute—however personally edifying its potential—but it must be pointed out that discussion is the precursor to understanding and spiritual growth.

Disagreements can be likened to rainstorms in the sense that while we would rather they not disrupt our day, they are nevertheless indispensable to the growth and well-being of the planet upon which we depend for our very existence. When viewed within the grander perspective (i.e., the macrocosm) that is Tao, disagreement or argument often serves to sow the seeds of understanding and to cultivate fresh ideas and concepts from the garden of our mind, resulting in new insights, concept relationships, and spiritual awareness.

The Jeffs of the world, however, refuse to look at the grand perspective—the forest, as it were—for fear of losing sight of the trees. They are the archetypes of the microcosmic perspective. Their minds are made up on specific subjects well in advance, and therefore, they are quite impervious to the viewpoints of other individuals, however accurate or well reasoned such positions may be. Further, since such individuals believe that they have all the answers already, they really aren't interested in seeking any further insight or understanding so much as they are in winning people over to their particular point of view.

But winning, per se, should never be the aim of any discussion. Instead, one should focus on learning, on expanding one's own understanding of the ways of life. The desire to win actually goes against the grain of Tao, as it creates a false dualism—an instant separation of winning and losing—with the result that our emphasis shifts from working to resolve our personal problems and expanding our current level of understanding, to the fear of losing and the necessity of winning at all costs.

As understanding and personal growth are ongoing, evolutionary processes, a position of "I know all that I need to know right now" goes against the grain of reality and only calls attention to the fact of an arrested cognitive development. Instead of actively seeking converts to a position of partial truth, we should instead seek to expand our understanding and to recognize the fact that knowledge, like life itself, is an ongoing process and never fixed at one point—or one point of view—in time. Truth, if that is what you are seeking to express, has no need of defenders—it simply is. To therefore take great pains to convey the obvious is folly, so why trouble yourself? As the *Tao te ching* says:

—81—

Wise men don't need to prove their point;
Men who need to prove their point aren't wise.[2]

In other words, those who insist on dominating conversation, who refuse to listen to evidence or points of view that are challenging or opposite to what they feel safe in believing, have thereby laid the foundation for dogma—

a position of close-mindedness that will stifle and eventually choke out any possibility of true learning. Bruce Lee pointed out the fallacy of such close-mindedness with one of his favorite stories; it tells of a Zen master who received a university professor who had come to inquire about Zen—and who was very much like our friend Jeff:

> *It was obvious to the master from the start of the conversation that the professor was not so much interested in learning about Zen as he was in impressing the master with his own opinions and knowledge. As the Zen teacher explained, the learned man would frequently interrupt him with remarks like "Oh, yes, we have that, too" and so on.*
>
> *Finally, the Zen teacher stopped talking and began to serve tea to the learned man. He poured the cup full, then kept pouring until the cup overflowed.*
>
> *"Enough!" the learned man once more interrupted. "The cup is overfull, no more will go in!"*
>
> *"Indeed, I see," answered the Zen teacher. "Like this cup, you are full of your own opinions and speculations. If you do not first empty your cup, how can you taste my cup of tea?"*

The need for an empty cup, or an open mind, shall serve as our metaphysical starting point. Let us assume for the moment that we in the West do not have all the answers. Let us begin with a blank slate, with no preconceived ideas, biases, opinions, or prejudices that will influence our judgment or impede our attempt at acquiring a new understanding on the ways of the world.

CHAPTER THREE

THE WAYS OF THE WORLD

Bruce Lee observed that very little about life is static. The internal state of the human body, for example, is constantly changing; new cells replace old cells in a never-ending process that appears to us as highly dynamic and in constant flux. Yet despite this phenomenon, the body has a certain balance, or inner immutability, that is as

The concept of the Tao was heavily ingrained in everything Bruce Lee did, from filmmaking and personal essays to his beliefs about combat and his artistic sketches.

important to our survival as change itself. Our bodies strive to keep our temperature fixed at 98.6 degrees and our blood pressure within certain parameters while constantly dealing with the profound cellular changes that occur on a daily or monthly basis, as well as those that are taking place from moment to moment.

These changes are the result of various influences upon our bodies, both external and internal, that impinge upon us from before we are born until the moment we die. These influences can take the form of such things as pain, joy, heat, cold, emotional conflict, muscular activity, and so on, and their varied forms are what constantly threaten to disrupt our internal balance or what American physiologist Walter B. Cannon termed "homeostasis" (from the Greek *homios*, meaning "similar," and *stasis*, meaning "position"). Ironically, while our bodies strive to maintain this condition of homeostasis, the nature of the process entails change as a prerequisite to its achievement. This brings about an apparent paradox: a condition of *change* being indispensable in order for an organism to remain *changeless*. Bruce Lee once made the observation that *"to change with change is the changeless state."*

It is a condition of "changeless change" that is the true state of our bodies, internal environment. Lee's aphorism serves to underscore the principle of *Yin/Yang*, or the interdependency of apparent opposites, as the sine qua non for the survival of our bodies (which we'll get into in greater detail in our next chapter). Our bodies, however, are simply reflections in miniature of the natural laws that regulate the ebb and flow of the cosmic universe of which they are a part. This being the case, it becomes possible for us to learn to understand the way of the world without by taking a look at the way of the world within.

To this end, Lao-tzu (circa 600 B.C.), the legendary founder of Taoism, made this observation:

—47—

One may know the world without going out of doors.
One may see the Way of Heaven without looking through the windows.[1]

When we look at the way of the world within, we cannot help but observe that change is an integral force there. Such factors as blood gases, hormone levels, electrolyte balances, fluid levels, pH balances, blood sugar, and other more complex processes are constantly shifting and adapting to the vicissitudes of life in order to preserve the internal balance and existence of our physical bodies. Such a dynamic inner state of our organism further results in unceasing changes in our emotions, impulses, sense of well-being, and even our spiritual perspectives. As this phenomenon of change within is merely a reflection of a much greater universal process without, it should not surprise us to learn that its metaphysical nature has been observed and theorized about by both Eastern and Western philosophers for centuries.

The pre-Socratic philosopher Heraclitus (circa 500 B.C.), for example, once wrote: "All things flow; nothing abides."[2] Heraclitus was referring to the ultimate reality of the external universe, which, as we've seen, operates under the identical laws governing our own physical bodies. It is upon this metaphysical observation of flux as constant—that is to say, of both our inner and outer universe being comprised of multitudinous phenomena of varying polarity—that we can come to better understand the true nature, or way, of the world that surrounds us.

However, this innocent observation is where the mutuality of cultural perspectives ends. Bruce Lee subscribed to a very ancient world view that, to Westerners raised in a Judeo-Christian tradition, is very foreign indeed: the fundamental Chinese Taoist and Indian Buddhist belief of how the world came into being. In these disciplines, it is held that the world came into existence not through a step-by-step process of creation much like one would follow if constructing a house or a model airplane, but rather by something that happened spontaneously, much like the way a flower suddenly blossoms. We were not *placed* into this world—we simply *grew* out of it.

This particular form of organic—as opposed to constructive—activity is commonly represented in Eastern art by a many-armed and many-headed divine figure, such as the Tibetan figure of Avalokitesvara, on whom the Chinese goddess Kwan-yin is based. Kwan-yin is sometimes known as the Goddess of Mercy (a distinctly Chinese belief, incidentally, as Kwan-yin became a goddess figure only when she reached China), although the original meaning of the figure is as a representation of the process and power of nature as earlier described.

The interesting thing about Kwan-yin is that she is depicted as having three faces and up to a thousand arms. The average Westerner might be tempted to make a snide comment regarding the enormous problem of coordination that so many appendages would have to present—while remaining completely oblivious to the fact that we encounter no less of a problem in simply being alive and going about our business day to day. As we've seen, our own bodies are able to self-regulate change into a state of apparent changelessness by performing all manner of incredibly complex functions simultaneously—and yet we never once have to stop and think about each individual aspect, process, or function, the sum total of which accounts for our daily existence. In a related vein, the renowned Zen author, Alan Watts (1915–1973), recounted the story of the centipede in his popular book *The Way of Zen*:

> The centipede was happy, quite,
> Until a toad in fun
> Said, "Pray, which leg goes after which?"
> This worked his mind to such a pitch,
> He lay distracted in a ditch,
> Considering how to run.[3]

Bruce Lee was fond of relating this fable (see Chapter 11, "Jeet Kune Do—the Quantum Perspective") to illustrate that the same thing could happen to us if we sought to understand the ways of the world solely by means of analysis or self-conscious processes. Lee often pointed out that pausing to analyze what we are doing develops a negative condition of what he termed "psychical stoppage." If, for example, we pause to consider how our respiratory system works every time we draw breath or how our central nervous system relays electrical impulses—or even if we stop to analyze the more mundane things to which we've grown accustomed in some mechanical way, such as knitting or tying a necktie—we will, like the centipede, become lost in a labyrinth of thought, with the result that we are unable to perform even the simplest of tasks. Lee elaborated on this concept by citing a passage from Daisetz T. Suzuki's *Zen and Japanese Culture* that contained a metaphor involving Kwan-yin:

Kwan-yin, the Goddess of Mercy, is sometimes represented with up to 1,000 arms, each holding a different instrument. If her mind stops with the use,

for instance, of a spear, all the other arms (999) will be of no use whatso-
ever. It is only because of her mind not stopping with the use of one arm,
but moving from one instrument to another, that all her arms prove useful
with the utmost degree of efficiency. Thus the figure is meant to demon-
strate that when the ultimate truth is realized, even as many as 1,000 arms
on one body may each be serviceable in one way or another.[4]

Thus, the Westerner might ask this: "How is it possible for Kwan-yin, this Goddess of Mercy, to use so many arms, faces, and eyes?" This is really tantamount to asking, "How can the centipede effectively use so many legs?" or "How do I make my body function with so many seemingly unrelated parts of it working together at once without my ever having to consciously think about this process at all?" Bruce Lee's answer to all of these questions would be that such processes are not governed by any means of conscious thought, but rather by a process that is itself self-governed.

Lee's perspective was that the natural order of things is more like a process of democracy than a monarchy. In a monarchy, we obviously have one political focal point, one central authority telling all the other members of its constituency what to do. In a democratic system, however, there exists something very much like a living organism. It is a process that is self-governing, or self-regulating, wherein all manner of different parts continue to develop and change independently and yet function together in terms of a harmonious pattern of Tao, of which Lao-tzu once said:

—34—
The great Tao flows everywhere.
All things are born from it,
yet it doesn't create them.
It pours itself into its work,
yet it makes no claim.
It nourishes infinite worlds,
yet it doesn't hold on to them.
Since it is merged with all things
and hidden in their hearts,
it can be called humble.

Since all things vanish into it
and it alone endures,
it can be called great.
It isn't aware of its greatness;
thus it is truly great.[5]

Thus is conceived the idea of an *ultimate reality* that does not govern the universe by ruling it—by telling it what to do—but by, as it were, allowing it the freedom to organize itself harmoniously. In other words, it is characteristic of Tao that while it is everywhere and in everything, giving life to all, it is never possessive or dictatorial. Tao is indifferent and unconditional, which is, in effect, the measure of its greatness. By extension, such qualities are the measure of greatness in those individuals who follow its example and accept things as they are without seeking personal gain or using others as a means to their ends. In fact, this is the only meaningful way in which greatness in human beings can realistically be measured.

Living: The Oneness of Things

Fast-forwarding from the creation of the world to August 7, 1993, I was asked to cover an event at Superior Galleries in Beverly Hills, California, for *Black Belt* magazine. It was called "The Bruce Lee Collection," and it marked the first time ever that many of Bruce Lee's personal writings were made public. One of the most incredible papers auctioned off that day, from a philosophical point of view, was an essay Lee had penned in the early 1960s while attending school in Seattle, Washington.

Lee had entitled the piece "Living: the Oneness of Things," and it perfectly encapsulated his views on the problems inherent in the Western philosophical approach as contrasted with the Eastern way of looking at life. In trying to discern Lee's beliefs regarding the ways of the world or in determining the nature of ultimate reality (what philosophy professors like to refer to as metaphysics), this essay proves a wonderful place to start, as Lee speaks of his axiomatic concepts and the nature of interdependent relationships:

Everything does have a real relationship, a mutuality in which the subject creates the object just as much as the object creates the subject. Thus the knower no longer feels himself to be separated from the known; the experiencer no longer feels himself to stand apart from the experience. Consequently, the whole notion of getting something OUT OF LIFE, of seeking FROM experience, becomes absurd. To put it in another way, it becomes vividly clear that in concrete fact I have no other self than the ONENESS of things of which I am aware.

The Moon in the Water

To better illustrate the concept of the harmony of universal relationships, Lee cited Alan Watts' famous "moon in the water" analogy, which indicated the interdependence of all things. This might rightly be considered the first lesson to be learned in our quest to understand our place in the universe. The analogy reveals that we are not simply isolated entities that stand apart from the universe, but are instead dynamic components *of* it, facets of the much greater whole—an active and capable part of the totality through which nature's power flows.

The phenomenon of the moon in the water is likened to human experience. The water is the subject and the moon the object. When there is no water, there is no moon in the water, and likewise when there is no moon. But when the moon rises the water does not wait to receive its image, and when even the tiniest drop of water is poured out the moon does not wait to cast its reflection. The moon does not intend to cast its reflection and the water does not receive its image on purpose. The event is caused as much by the water as by the moon, and as the water manifests the brightness of the moon, the moon manifests the clarity of the water. Everything does have a real relationship. . . .[6]

There exists in Western logic a rule entitled the law of identity or the excluded middle, which states that things are what they are ("A is A") and that it is impossible for one thing *to be* and *not to be* something in the same space and time. To the Eastern mind, however, this *either/or* way of looking at life is inaccurate; it is indeed possible for something to be opposite and yet the same. Within our species, for example, exist both man and woman—opposites one would think—and yet they are the same in as much as they are both human beings. In fact, man and woman are not so much opposites as they are complementaries; divided in such a fashion as to be able to reproduce themselves with their union. Man and woman, then, are the legs upon which the life of our species stands, and when one half is absent, the whole perishes.

Our bodies, as we've seen, are only able to evolve owing to the fact that they are comprised of processes that are at once both changing and changeless. By extension, the universe consists of a similar relationship of complementaries, the nature of which is akin to change and stasis, front and back, short and tall, loud and quiet, and hard and soft. These things arise mutually and are experienceable solely in terms of their being aspects—or poles—of the same universal process, much as positive and negative are different poles of the same magnetic system.

Our universe is so interconnected in all of its parts that one part of it, so-called, can exist only in relation to all the others. All motion, too, exists only in relation to all other motion. It works—in the terminology of the physical sciences—as a field of forces. There is no separate center in which any motion or activity originates. All activity that occurs in any spot, as it were, originates over the whole system.

A problem arises, however, when we develop excessive self-consciousness, feeling ourselves to be somehow separate or independent from this process. That is to say, we develop an excessive sensation of distance between the experiencer and the experience, and then we try to make the one latch on to the other completely and attempt to control it. In other words, there is a breakdown when the experiencer resists the experience, thereby causing the whole pattern of our consciousness to turn on itself. In such conditions—such as when we worry or worry about worrying by saying to ourselves such things as "I must relax!" or "I must not think that way!"—life can become an almost intolerable burden to many.

It is largely for this reason that the philosophy espoused by Bruce Lee offers a way of deliverance from the vicious circle of life that has been brought about by thousands of years of Western theorizing. But having said this, any conscious attempt at extrication—of *trying* to get out—is still working on the assumption that there is a real experiencer to be, as it were, extracted from the experience, and that, as we've seen, is an illusion. There is no experiencer to be *extracted from*, or who can *escape from*, experience. There is simply *experiencing*. Much like Alan Watts' statement that "the purpose of dancing is to dance," the purpose of life is to live—which is simply another way of stating that it is an *experiential* process.

The point to be drawn from all of this is that you should not get so caught up in analyzing the world around you and searching for hidden cause-and-effect relationships that you end up standing apart from it for the purpose of analysis. According to Bruce Lee: *"People do not live conceptually or scientifically defined lives, for the essential quality of living life lies simply in the living."*

To better illustrate this concept, let us assume that you are watching a beautiful sunset on a tranquil evening. The scene and the whole experience fills you with a tremendous sense of peace and inner calm. Suddenly, however, you sit bolt upright thinking to yourself: "Something's missing here! Could it be that maybe I could be experiencing even more comfort than I am right now? I'll bet there's a way to make this a *better* scenario. What if I were watching this sunset from a nice screened-in porch on a mild August night on the shore of a lake in northern Ontario? I've heard that those northern Canadian sunsets are really spectacular! I'd better call my travel agent when I get back to the office on Monday and. . . ."

The problem here is obvious. You can become so wrapped up in thinking of ways to "maximize" your *future* enjoyment potential that you'll make it impossible to experience the present joy at all. As the present is all that exists (the past having expired and the future not yet born), the present is truly all that we should be concerned with. The *now* is all that can affect us. Bruce Lee believed that if you were in the midst of a life experience such as enjoying yourself, you should accept it for what it is. Enjoy *living* and experiencing the *now*, and don't try to pause or analyze the situation by stepping out or away from the moment in order to see if you are getting the utmost out of it:

The essential quality of living life lies simply in the living. Do not, as when in the midst of enjoying yourself, step out for a moment and examine your-

self to see if you are getting the utmost out of the occasion. Or not content with feeling happy, you want to feel yourself feeling happy—so as to be sure not to miss anything. Living exists when life lives THROUGH us—unhampered in its flow, for he who is living is not conscious of living, and in this is the life IT lives.

In other words, simply let life—with all of its experiences—flow through you. As Johannes Jacobus van der Leeuw (1893–1934), the prominent Dutch theosophical writer once said: "The meaning of life is not a problem to be solved, but a reality to be experienced."

This is precisely what Bruce Lee was driving at. So how does one experience living in life's suchness? How do we free ourselves of the bonds of self-consciousness so that we can enjoy the experience of becoming moment to moment? According to Lee, the answer lies in letting go of the ego, and that, in turn, entails a process of rigorous self-examination until, bit by bit, the superficial layers of "you" are peeled away to reveal only the irreducible—real—you. As Bruce Lee once revealed to Daniel Lee:

More and more, Dan, I mean it's becoming more and more simple to me as a human being. And more and more I search [within] myself, and more and more the questions are more and more listed. And more and more I see clearly [that it's a matter of simplicity]. It is, it really is. What it is is that what man has to get over is the consciousness—the consciousness of himself. . . . a realization in this regard as to whatever your pursuit might be. In my case, the pursuit of becoming moment to moment—whatever that thing is—and constantly questioning myself: What is this, Bruce? Is it true or is it not true? Do you really mean it or not mean it? Once I've found that out, that's it.

In fact, during a private lesson with actor James Coburn that appears in the martial arts training film *Bruce Lee's Jeet Kune Do,* Bruce Lee in a voice-over makes the observation that his pupil is being too self-conscious about executing a particular technique, with the result that he keeps missing his mark. He tells Coburn: "You are trying too much to control the movement, and by too much control, you're too concerned about its execution. Therefore you're too tight."

Lee instructs his student to relax mentally, not to worry about how to plant his foot, how to torque his body, or when to raise his leg. In other words, he encourages Coburn to *get over the consciousness of himself.* Heeding Lee's advice, Coburn drops all conscious effort, emptying his mind of all analysis and leaves the technique alone to, as it were, complete itself. Sure enough, Coburn's very next kick hits the target perfectly, almost effortlessly— and with maximum impact, causing Lee to remark: "You see? Right on the target! When you ease the burden of your mind, you just do it."

This concept was further illuminated in Lee's essay:

Life lives; and in the living flow—no questions are raised. The reason is that life is a living NOW! Completeness, the now, is an absence of the conscious mind to strive to divide that which is indivisible. For once the completeness of things is taken apart, it is no longer complete. All the pieces of a car that has been taken apart may be there, but it is no longer a car in its original nature, which is its function or life. So in order to live life wholeheartedly, the answer is life simply IS.

The Failure of Western Philosophy

If life, then, is an experiential rather than an analytical phenomenon, this would explain why so many people who earnestly seek peace of mind or contentment come away frustrated and confused from their forays into Western philosophy, with its emphasis on analysis and then additional analysis of further analysis (recall Wittgenstein's labyrinth of propositions and subpropositions from the last chapter). This, as we've seen, is not only unnecessary but, according to Bruce Lee, ultimately self-defeating:

In life, we accept naturally the full reality of what we see and feel in general with no shadow of a doubt. Western philosophy, however, does not accept what life believes, and strives to convert reality into a problem. Like asking such questions as: "Is this chair that I see in front of me really there? Can it exist by itself?" Thus, rather than making life easy for living by living in accord with life, Western philosophy complicates it by replacing the world's tranquillity with the restlessness of problems. It is like asking a person how he breathes—this will immediately choke the breath out of him when he attempts to think about the process. Why try to arrest and interrupt the flow of life? Why create such fuss? A person simply breathes.

In a nutshell, the problem with the Western approach is that it attempts to *explain* life as opposed to revealing how to *experience* it. In other words, there is experiencing and there is theorizing, and the two are mutually exclusive, existing in an inverse ratio to one another; that is, the more time you spend *theorizing,* the less time is left for you *experientially.* The problem with theorizing, according to Bruce Lee, is that its very foundation is settled upon the denial of reality by attempting to talk about it, to go *around* it, to catch anything that attracts our intellect and abstract it *away* from reality itself. He noted:

Thus Western philosophy begins by saying that the outside world is not a basic fact, that its existence can be doubted and that every proposition in which the reality of the outside world is affirmed is not an evident proposition but one which needs to be divided, dissected, and analyzed—it is to stand consciously aside and try to square a circle.

Western philosophy, then, is for the most part not really concerned with the issue of living qua living but rather in the construction of an activity concerning theoretic knowledge. Most Western philosophers are not as interested in living—in its purest sense—as they are in trying to theorize about living. This inclination is not conducive to either enjoying or experiencing the ultimate reality of life, but rather to an austere and detached contemplation of it. As Lee once observed, *"To contemplate a thing implies maintaining oneself* OUTSIDE *it, resolved to keep a distance between it and ourselves."*

This is not what our world view should be if happiness and true comprehension of the ways of the world are to be our goals. We must not dissect and hyperanalyze. We must simply open ourselves to experience and, by so doing, serve as a conduit through which the reality of living is made manifest in our every move, thought, action, and experience of the moment.

Interestingly enough, Bruce Lee's view of the world is one that has been verified in recent years by modern physics. According to current scientists, the basic building blocks of existence are not matter—in the traditional sense of the term—but rather probabilities, dynamic yet interrelated patterns of energy. Thus, ultimately our universe is composed, not of waves or particles, but something in between.

David Bohm, the Professor Emeritus of Physics at the University of London and the author of such books as *Quantum Theory, Causality and Chance in Modern Physics,* and *Wholeness and the Implicate Order,* has advanced the idea of an "implicate order" in describing the universe as a type of hologram in which the parts are themselves reflections and embodiments of the greater whole. In Fritjof Capra's book *The Turning Point: Science, Society, and the Rising Culture,* a discussion of the S-matrix theory indicates that our universe is "a dynamic web of interrelated events." According to Bruce Lee:

> We are vortices whose center is a point that is motionless and eternal but which appears in manifestation as motion which increases in velocity in the manner of a whirlpool or tornado (whose epicenter is still) from nucleus to periphery. The nucleus is in reality, whereas the vortex is a phenomenon in the form of a multidimensional force field—HOLD TO THE CORE.

It is in this observation—of the universe as one inseparable, interrelated field—that Lee's philosophy bears, perhaps, the most serious consideration:

> The world is seen as an inseparably interrelated field, no part of which can actually be separated from the other (there would be no bright stars without dim stars, and without the surrounding darkness, no stars at all). Oppositions have become mutually cooperative instead of mutually exclusive, and there is no longer any conflict between the individual man and nature.

To fully understand this concept of the indivisibility of being, and its application to our lives, we will first need to become familiar with another principle that we touched upon earlier and that is integral to Bruce Lee's philosophy. This is the principle of dynamic balance or, as it is more commonly symbolized, Yin/Yang.

CHAPTER FOUR

ON YIN/YANG

*N*eo-Confucianism had a profound impact upon Chinese thought and, in time, upon Bruce Lee. The writings of one of the Neo-Confucianists (in fact, the man considered to be the movement's pioneer), Chou Tun-i (also called Chou Lien-ch'i and Chou Lien-hsi, 1017–1073), held particular import.

Chou Tun-i wrote two short treatises, *T'ai-chi-t'u shuo* (an explanation of the diagram of the Great Ultimate) and *T'ung-shu* ("Penetrating the Book of Changes") that served to assimilate certain key aspects of Taoist philosophy with Confucian thought.

The *T'ai Chi* ("Great Ultimate") diagram, or symbol, is what we in the West have taken to calling the "Yin/Yang symbol," as it serves to encompass the "one in the many" philosophy of Yin/Yang.

According to the history of the Great Ultimate diagram, the Great Ultimate through movement creates Yang. When Yang reaches its limit, the movement becomes tranquil, which generates Yin. This alternation of movement and tranquillity creates Yin and Yang, which, in turn, give birth to the Five Agents of Water, Fire, Wood, Metal, and Earth. These Five Agents constitute one vast interdependent system of Yin/Yang, and Yin/Yang constitutes the Great Ultimate.

According to Chou Tun-i: "The many are [ultimately] one, and the one is actually differentiated into the many," and "the one and many each has its own correct state of being."[1]

This was a philosophical precept that Bruce Lee would eventually find much solace and truth in. Lee went on record in the early part of 1962 as indicating that he began learning gung fu at age thirteen, for the same reasons that most of us take up a martial art, simply because he "wanted to learn how to fight." However, once he started his martial arts training in earnest, Lee soon learned that combat and hard physical training were only one part of a rather complex process. The other part consisted of understanding, tolerance, and peace of mind—and it was by far the more difficult of the two aspects to cultivate. Nevertheless, Lee persisted and, in time, came to possess a much broader understanding of not only the combative elements of gung fu, but also of its philosophical underpinning of Yin/Yang, causing him to comment to a reporter in 1962:

> It has changed my whole life, and I have a completely different way of thinking. Gung fu is a way of life as well as a mode of self-defense. It is based on Yin (negative) and Yang (positive), where everything is a complement. Examples are softness with firmness, night with day, and man with woman. It is a quiet awareness of one's opponent's strength and plans, and how to complement them.

While many of us in the West are familiar with the Yin/Yang symbol, few are familiar with what the symbol actually represents. In this respect, let us return once more to the words of Bruce Lee to illuminate this ancient philosophical principle:

> Gung fu is based on the symbol of the Yin and Yang, a pair of mutually complementary and interdependent forces that act continuously, without cessation, in this universe. . . . The Yin and Yang are two interlocking complementaries. Etymologically the characters of Yin and Yang mean darkness and light. The ancient character of Yin, the dark part of the circle, is a drawing of clouds and hill. Yin can represent anything in the universe as negativeness, passiveness, gentleness, internal, insubstantiality, femaleness, moon, darkness, night, etc. The other complementary half of the circle is Yang. The lower part of the character signifies slanting sunrays, while the upper part represents the sun. Yang can represent anything as positiveness, activeness, firmness, external substantiality, maleness, sun, brightness, day, etc. The common mistake of most martial artists is to identify these two forces as Yin and Yang, as dualistic (thus the so-called soft style and the firm style). But Yin/Yang is one inseparable force of one

unceasing interplay of movement. They are conceived of as essentially one, or as two coexisting forces of one indivisible whole. They are not cause and effect but should be looked at as sound and echo, or light and shadow. If this "oneness" is viewed as two separate entities, realization of the ultimate reality of gung fu won't be achieved.

Let's consider this principle in a little greater depth. According to Bruce Lee, the basic theory of Yin/Yang is that: *"there is nothing in the universe so permanent as never to change."*

To Lee, this meant that we are all part of a universal process of growth and evolution, brought into being from the unceasing interplay of Yin/Yang. Our bodies, for example, are composed of billions of cells—each and every one of which is composed of microscopic constituents whirling in ever-changing orbits of incessant energy. They are, in effect, miniature universes unto themselves and are evolving and interchanging with one another continuously. Bruce Lee once wrote: *"The flow of movements is in their interchangeability."* He also said: *"The stillness in stillness is not the real stillness. Only when there is stillness in movement does the universal rhythm manifest."*

This unceasing interchangeability of Yin/Yang was symbolically illustrated by Lee when he placed two revolving arrows around the Yin/Yang symbol to represent the principles underlying his martial art of jeet kune do. In other words, the arrows represented that all apparent opposites arise out of one unified force. As he himself once stated:

The emblem of Lee's jeet kune do school employed the Yin/Yang symbol with two arrows encircling it, emphasizing the interdependency of all things. Surrounding the symbol in Chinese characters is the phrase "Using no way as way; having no limitation as limitation."

I was asked by a so-called Chinese kung fu instructor once—one of those that really looked the part, with beard and all—as to what I think of Yin (gentle) and Yang (firm). I simply answered: "Baloney!" Of course he was quite shocked to hear my answer and still has not come to the realization that it is never two.

Lee then went on to explain:

We must realize then that it is not a matter of the soft versus the firm, because as I've pointed out, gentleness and firmness are always part of one whole and are equally important as well as unavoidably interdependent on each other. If one rejects either the firm or the soft, this will lead to separation, and separation will run to extreme. Those who cling to either extreme are known as either "physically bound" or "intellectually bound," though the former are more bearable. At least the "physically bound" do struggle.

This fundamental principle of the unity and interdependency of apparent opposites results in a condition of "changeless change," which has its referent in almost every culture. Heraclitus, for example, the pre-Socratic philosopher whom we met in the previous chapter, once said: "One cannot step twice into the same river."[2]

By this he meant that because a river is constantly flowing, with new waters flowing into it from upstream, it is never static and cannot ever be the "same" river that it was when you first stepped into it. Common opinion supposes that what it calls "the river" is something that will endure—statically—for a time. But the river, according to Heraclitus, remains in such a state for no time at all. In fact, it has changed while you have said its name.

Thus, in a more personal sense, it is with ourselves, as we are simply microcosms of the macrocosmic flow. This, too, is a greater reflection of the harmony of apparent opposites, or Yin/Yang. While we ourselves and the universe within which we exist change on a daily, almost imperceptible basis, this process of changing with the subtle changes of the universe is a changeless phenomenon that has been ongoing since the beginning of time. Again, recall the words of Bruce Lee from the previous chapter: *"To change with change is the changeless state."*

More to the point, this principle of constant evolutionary flow implies that all things—not just rivers that ran through ancient Greece—are subject to change. In our case, we are never the same people we once were. With each passing year, our bodily tissues renew through the process of metabolism, creating in our bodies new cells to replace the older ones. In other words, everything in our universe (both inner and outer) flows in an intricate relationship to what, ostensibly, would appear to be its opposite: birth begets death, day begets night, rise complements fall, male complements female, and so on. The nature of the relationship is such that they contradict as well as complement each other. For example, if activity reaches its extreme point, it must become inactivity, which forms Yin. Extreme inactivity, on the other hand, returns to become activity, which is Yang. Thereby, one condition becomes the cause of the other, and vice versa.

The principle of complementary and simultaneous increasing and decreasing goes on in perpetuity, and while these forces would appear to be in direct conflict with one another, they are in reality mutually dependent. Instead of opposition, there is cooperation and alternation. This is precisely why the Yin/Yang symbol has within each of its halves a small circle that is the color of the opposite half. Within the half that is Yin this small circle represents Yang, and vice versa. This serves to symbolize the fact that Yin and Yang interact with each other in an endless succession of changes. Within even the most masculine of men, there is a feminine component, and within woman resides a small part that is unquestionably male.

The Yin/Yang, or T'ai Chi, is an immensely interesting and descriptive symbol, as it signifies that all things in nature are an interrelated part of a greater totality—however independent or individual they might appear. Lao-tzu wrote of it thusly:

—II—

We join spokes together in a wheel,
but it is the center hole
that makes the wagon move.

We shape clay into a pot,
but it is the emptiness inside
that holds whatever we want.

> We hammer wood for a house,
> but it is the inner space
> that makes it livable.
>
> We work with being,
> but non-being is what we use.[3]

Bruce Lee addressed this phenomenon in his writings:

In reality, things are "whole" and cannot be separated into two parts. When I say the heat makes me perspire, the heat and perspiring are just one process as they are coexistent and the one could not exist but for the other. If a person riding a bicycle wishes to go somewhere, then he cannot pump on both the pedals at the same time or not pump on them at all. In order to go forward, he has to pump on one pedal and release the other. So the movement of going forward requires this "oneness" of pumping and releasing. Pumping is the result of releasing and vice versa, each being the cause and result of the other. Things do have their complementaries, and complementaries coexist. Instead of mutually exclusive, they are mutually dependent and are a function each of the other.

Lee then went on to explain the significance of the Yin/Yang symbol:

In the Yin/Yang symbol there is a white spot on the black part and a black spot on the white one. This is to illustrate the balance in life, for nothing can survive long by going to either extreme, be it pure Yin (gentleness) or pure Yang (firmness). Notice that the stiffest tree is most easily cracked, while the bamboo or willow survive by bending with the wind.

In life, Lee noticed that the Western approach was often to confront things head on—in other words, to be Yang or firm about things. This approach, if adopted repeatedly in dealing with life's vicissitudes, can lead to problems: *"The American is [typically] like an oak tree—he stands firm against the wind. If the wind is strong, he cracks. The Oriental [prefers to] stand like bamboo, bending with the wind and springing back when the wind ceases—stronger than ever before."*

In other words, instead of opposing the natural patterns of the universe, it is far more productive to learn to flow and blend with them.

The Law of Harmony

Bruce Lee taught that the application of the principles of Yin/Yang are expressed as the law of harmony. This law indicates that one should be in harmony with, as opposed to rebellion against, the strength and force of nature. In other words, one should do nothing that is not natural or spontaneous; the key tenet being not to strain in any way. In terms of combating an opponent, Lee explained the law of harmony thusly:

> *When opponent A uses strength (Yang) on B, B must not resist him . . . with strength; in other words, do not use positiveness (Yang) against positiveness (Yang) but instead yield to him with softness (Yin) and lead him to the direction of his own force, negativeness (Yin) to positiveness (Yang). When A's strength goes to the extreme, the positiveness (Yang) will change to negativeness (Yin), B then taking him at his unguarded moment and attacking with force (Yang). Thus the whole process is [never] unnatural or strained. B fits his movement harmoniously and continuously into that of A without resisting or striving.*

Lee liked to illustrate this principle in relation to martial art, but you can see the law of harmony present in many different areas. Consider the case of Brenda: She has been a yo-yo dieter for years. Not that she consumed yo-yos, you understand, but she's caught in a never-ending cycle of fad diets and returning body fat. Brenda always diets too severely in an effort to "force" (Yang) her body into a state of complying (Yin) with a mental picture she has of how she thinks she ought to "ideally" appear. In fact, none of her friends can remember a time when she wasn't on a diet—and yet she has been overweight for as long as they've known her.

Unfortunately, poor Brenda is doomed to disappointment because she goes to extremes—either total deprivation (Yin) or total gorging (Yang). If she had adopted a more natural position of moderation, she would have obtained the body of her dreams long ago and without anywhere near the labors and travails she's been putting herself through. Bruce Lee believed that the pendulum of life required balance, and in Brenda's case, she would have been far more successful simply eating a more modest, well-balanced diet.

In the realm of bodybuilding, I knew several iron pumpers who used to cut out all of their carbohydrate intake prior to a contest in order to make their muscles appear more defined. And it worked—for a while. Immediately after the contest, however, these bodybuilders would invariably become as fat as prize hogs because their bodies were craving that component of a well-balanced diet that had been denied—the carbohydrates. When their biology could no longer be suppressed, it kicked back in with a vengeance. The bodybuilders would then literally gorge themselves to the point of discomfort in order to satiate their inner cravings. You see, their bodies didn't know that they were simply being temporarily deprived of this essential macronutrient for cosmetic purposes; from the body's perspective, it was starving! After all, the human brain and central nervous system derive 99.9 percent of the nutrition they need to function efficiently from glucose, which is simply the form that carbohydrates take when broken down in the liver and released into the bloodstream. In fact, if the body doesn't receive glucose via carbohydrate as a result of a balanced diet, it will create its own by breaking down an amino acid called alanine and converting it into glucose. Again, the pendulum of life must have balance. Extreme nutritional habits are at odds with the principle of Yin/Yang, which is, as we've seen, the way of the world.

The same principle applies to going to extremes in discussion. If, for example, you're having an argument with a spouse, and he's becoming heated and irate, don't lash back with the same—respond with passiveness and kindness. Your mate's anger, requiring a high level of intensity to sustain itself, will soon burn out and give way to Yin or gentleness. Again, any extreme of Yin or Yang will ultimately lead to its complementary, so sit back and let nature take its course, content in the understanding that it will do so and that, again, "nothing is so permanent as never to change."

Quiescence, from Lee's perspective, was a kind of philosophical inaction, a refusal to interfere with the natural course of things. If resistance is encountered, the wiser course is not to quarrel, fight, or make war (as in the case of quarreling nations), but to retire silently, and to win, if at all, through yielding and patience. It has after all been noted that passivity has its victories more often than action. In other words, if you do not quarrel, no one on earth will be able to quarrel with you.

The Law of Noninterference

The principle of the law of harmony has as its corollary the law of noninterference with nature, which, according to Bruce Lee, taught a person to forget about himself and merely respond to what was happening before him, like echo to sound—with no deliberation. Again using martial art for illustrative purposes, Lee advanced the proposition as follows:

The basic idea is to defeat the opponent by yielding to him and using his own strength. That is why a gung fu man never asserts himself against his opponent, and never [puts himself] in frontal opposition to the direction of his [opponent's] force. When being attacked, he will not resist but will control the attack by swinging with it. This law illustrates the principles of nonresistance and nonviolence, which were founded on the idea that the branches of a fir tree snapped under the weight of the snow, while the simple reeds, weaker but more supple, can overcome it.

Bruce Lee also found profound and enduring truth in the words of Lao-tzu, the greatest of the pre-Confucian philosophers, who pointed out:

—78—

Nothing in the world
is as soft and yielding as water.
Yet for dissolving the hard and inflexible,
nothing can surpass it.

The soft overcomes the hard;
the gentle overcomes the rigid.
Everyone knows this is true,
but few can put it into practice.[4]

From this Bruce Lee concluded: *"Because he can yield, a man can survive. In contrast, the Yang principle, which is assumed to be rigorous and hard, makes a man break under pressure."*

It is interesting to note the value that Lao-tzu placed on the Yin principles of softness and pliableness, making them synonymous with life and survival. As we shall see in our next chapter, Bruce Lee believed that Lao-tzu was on to something when he said that we could come a long way toward understanding the essence of Tao by observing and understanding the nature of water.

CHAPTER FIVE
RUNNING WATER

Empty your mind. Be formless, shapeless, like water.
When you put water into a cup, it becomes the cup;
When you put water into a bottle, it becomes the bottle;
When you put water into a teapot, it becomes the teapot.
Now water can flow—or it can crash.
Be water, my friend.

BRUCE LEE

⌘

To some of you reading this book, the above quotation may seem an odd paean to things aqueous. However, I guarantee that by the time you have finished this chapter, this aphorism of Bruce Lee's will have taken on a new meaning entirely. To be able to flow like water with adversity until you are in position to overcome it, is one of the key tenets of Bruce Lee's philosophy—a philosophy that, until now, has been restricted solely to those individuals who were select students of Bruce Lee's personal form of martial art, jeet kune do. Even then, by no means did all of these individuals grasp the man's philosophic precepts with any degree of firmness, opting instead to keep Lee's teachings confined to the realm of hand-to-hand combat. This myopic view of Lee's contribution, indeed his true legacy, is unfortunate, because the teachings of Bruce Lee have so much more to offer than merely a practical prism through which to view a street fight.

Lee's martial philosophy, which he named jeet kune do (from the Cantonese, meaning "the way of the intercepting fist") deals with individualism, self-expression, and learning to adapt oneself instantly and harmoniously to whatever obstacle might stand in your path. Through this process of harmonious adaptation, Lee believed, one could overcome adversity—in any form. Lee's perspective was fresh, his insight into the human condition unique, and most important, the self-actualizing philosophy that he pioneered has continued to work flawlessly to the benefit of all who have chosen to apply it. But first, let us consider the significance of Lee's water analogy.

The Nature of Water

For centuries, the Chinese have held a healthy respect—indeed, a profound awe—for the nature of water. *The Kuan-tzu*, a collection of writings of Kuan Chung (d. 645), had this to say of this wondrous element:

Water is the blood of the earth, and flows through its veins. Therefore, it is said that water is something that has complete faculties. . . . It is accumulated in Heaven and Earth, and stored up in the various things [of the world]. It comes forth in metal and stone, and is concentrated in living creatures. Therefore it is said that water is something spiritual. . . . Hence the solution for the sage who would transform the world lies in water.[1]

So also in the writings of Chuang-tzu:

Still water is like glass.
You can look in it and see the bristles on your chin.
It is a perfect level;
A carpenter could use it.
If water is so clear, so level,
How much more the spirit of man?[2]

As we've seen, water was Lao-tzu's favorite symbol for the Tao:

—8—

The highest goodness, water-like
Does good to everything and goes
Unmurmuring to places men despise;
But so, is close in nature to the Way [Tao].[3]

To Bruce Lee, however, the nature of water revealed a different lesson entirely. When Lee was seventeen years old (one year shy of his leaving for the United States), he had a profound experience while sailing alone in a junk upon the sea that flows through Hong Kong's Victoria Harbor. It was the sea, itself, in fact, that contributed to Lee's experience of what the Chinese call *tun-wu*, (the Japanese, *satori*), the Zen equivalent of a sudden spiritual insight or awakening, causing him to believe that he had united with Tao—the Chinese term for the force underlying all of nature's ways. The experience changed Lee's life and most certainly his philosophy of life.

Bruce Lee (right) learning "the art of detachment" from his first—and only—sifu, professor Yip Man.

As it happened, Lee had spent the prior four years of his life at this point in arduous training in the art of Wing Chun, a branch of Chinese gung fu that stressed heavily the principle of gentleness in neutralizing your opponent's effort and minimizing your own expenditure of energy. The discipline lay not in resisting one's opponent with strength charging head-on into strength, but rather in learning how to understand and thereby utilize your opponent's force and energy to your own advantage—much like one must learn to use, not oppose, the forces of wind and water if one wishes to learn the art of effective sailing. In other words, the art of Wing Chun teaches its practitioners how to be their opponent's complementary, as opposed to adversary, through a process of calmness and nonstriving (which should be starting to sound familiar to you, dear reader, about now).

In any event, as simple as the concept sounded, Lee found that he was having some difficulty with its actual application. He found that the moment he engaged in combat with an opponent, his mind was angry and perturbed, which caused him to use force (Yang) against, rather than compliance (Yin) with, his opponent's techniques. After a series of blows, all that remained in his mind was to beat his opponent into the ground decisively.

Noticing that his young student was not understanding the lesson, Lee's instructor, an elderly Chinese gentleman by the name of Yip Man, approached and instructed him to relax:

"Forget about yourself and follow the opponent's movement," he told him.

"Let your mind do the countermovement without deliberation. Learn the art of detachment. Just relax."

"Aha," thought Lee. "That's the secret—I *must* relax!" But even the formulation of this thought had, in retrospect many years later, been an indication that he had, again, missed the point. As Lee was to later recall: *"Right there I had already done something contradictory against my will. That was when I said 'I must relax.' The demand for effort in 'must' was already inconsistent with the effortlessness in 'relax.'"*

As Lee's mounting frustration became apparent to his old instructor, he approached Lee again and offered the following advice: "Lee, follow nature and don't interfere with her ways. Never assert yourself against nature: never be in frontal opposition to any problem, but swing with it. Don't practice this week. Go home and think."

Such an admonition only made it impossible for Lee to do anything other than seethe. Still, he took his instructor's advice and stayed home the following week. After many hours of meditation, he gave up and decided to go sailing at sea alone in a junk. As his junk cut through the waves of the sea, he thought back on what his instructor had said to him and of his own inability to apply the principle of Yin properly. Suddenly his temper flared and he punched at the water with all of his might—and at that instant, he was availed of new insight:

> *Right then, at that moment, a thought suddenly struck me. Wasn't this water, the very basic stuff, the essence of gung fu? Didn't the common water just illustrate to me the [Yin] principle of gung fu? I struck it just now, but it did not suffer hurt. Again I stabbed at it with all my might, yet it was not wounded. I then tried to grasp a handful of it, but it was impossible. This water, the softest substance in the world, could fit itself into any container. Although it seemed weak, it could penetrate the hardest substances in the world. That was it! I wanted to be like the nature of water.*

But the lesson wasn't over yet. While still savoring the insight, Lee continued to gaze into the water when suddenly a seagull flew over, casting its reflection upon the waves. This was the moment of Lee's satori:

> *Right then as I was absorbing myself, another mystic sense of hidden meaning started upon me. Shouldn't it be the same, then, that the thoughts and emotions I had in front of an opponent pass like the reflection of the bird flying over the water? This was exactly what professor Yip meant by being detached. . . . In order to control myself, I must first accept myself by going with and not against my nature.*

Lee then lay back in the boat, feeling that he had united with Tao. He had become one with the ways of nature. Letting the boat drift freely, Lee just lay there, enjoying a state of inner harmony, realizing that what he had thought to be the many opposing forces of the world were in fact mutually cooperative instead of mutually exclusive. With this understanding, there was no longer any conflict in his mind: *"The whole world to me was unitary."*

This experience and the conclusion that Lee drew from it served to create his famous water analogy with which we opened this chapter. Lee would frequently evoke this analogy to illustrate the principle of Yin as it applied

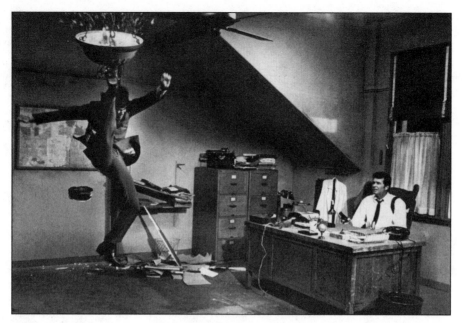

"Water can flow—or it can crash." Bruce Lee demonstrated the "crashing" component of the water principle while an amazed James Garner looks on during a scene from the movie Marlowe *(1969).*

to facing adversity or combating force. Lee observed that water was so malleable that it was impossible to grasp a handful of it, and that when struck, it was impossible to hurt. It was at once both pure Yin, by virtue of the fact that it remained one of the softest, most yielding substances in the world, and pure Yang, in that it was also capable of penetrating the hardest forms of matter. It could be calm, like the still surface of a pond, or turbulent and violent, like Niagara Falls.

The nature of water, then, is to adapt itself instantly to any obstacle in its path and, by moving at its own pace, begin a natural process of surmounting it. In other words, the lesson to be learned from water is that if we can learn to flow with adversity, we will eventually overcome it. Additionally, it is only through our flowing with life that we are able to adapt and grow. Indeed, life is movement, with the result that if we cease to flow with it, it passes us by. As Bruce Lee said: *"Running water never grows stale. So you've got to just 'keep on flowing.'"*

The nature of water, Bruce Lee held, also revealed a philosophic corollary of Yin/Yang—that of the necessity of bending with adversity.

Part Two

Defeating Adversity

CHAPTER SIX

BEND AND SURVIVE

*I*n August 1972, Bruce Lee was in the midst of fleshing out a concept for his fourth film. The film was to be titled *The Game of Death*, and the concept he intended to convey was the absolute necessity for human beings to be able to bend with adversity and thereby adapt to whatever circumstances beset them. Although the plot would apply this principle to the martial arts, to Lee it also stood as one of the fundamental principles of life:

> *At present I am working on the script for my next film. I haven't really decided on the title yet, but what I want to show is the necessity to adapt oneself to changing circumstances. The inability to adapt brings destruction. I already have the first scene in my mind. As the film opens, the audience sees a wide expanse of snow. Then the camera closes in on a clump of trees while the sounds of a strong gale fill the screen. There is a huge tree in the center of the screen, and it is all covered with thick snow. Suddenly there is a loud snap, and a huge branch of the tree falls to the ground. It cannot yield to the force of the snow so it breaks. Then the camera moves to a willow tree which is bending with the wind. Because it adapts itself to the environment, the willow survives.*

It should be noted that this principle of "bend and survive" is not taken to mean *complete yielding*, which is simply collapse or defeat, but rather to have *give*, or pliability. As Lee once wrote:

> *Be soft, yet not yielding.*
> *Be firm, yet not hard.*

This is a naturally occurring phenomenon that is present in almost every facet of existence, from snow-laden trees to man-made architecture. Take, for example, the bridges that we drive upon every day. If they did not possess this ability to bend or yield slightly, they would ultimately collapse. This capacity to yield (Yin), while often considered a "feminine" quality, is by no means a sign of weakness. In fact, it is instead a sign of great strength (Yang)—a quality traditionally considered masculine.

Once again we note that both Yin and Yang qualities are present here as different aspects of one and the same process. That the bridge is able to have the strength to endure (Yang) is based solely on its pliability (Yin). Such is the natural balance that is inherent in all things (we touched on this balance in Chapter 4). In fact, the quality of balance—or the nonextremist nature of Tao—is present in order that we might realize the ultimate expression of our true natures.

You can, for example, always be certain that when a man goes out of his way to convince you of his masculinity, he is suppressing the ultimate expression of his manhood. Likewise, when a woman attempts to act 100 percent "female," the ultimate expression of her womanhood is in jeopardy. This observation caused Lao-tzu to write the following passage sometime between the sixth and fifth century B.C.:

—28—

Knowing the male but keeping the female,
one becomes a universal stream.
Becoming a universal stream,
one is not separated from eternal virtue.[1]

In other words, if the male can allow himself to be weak, and if the female can allow herself to be strong, then both will be in accord with Tao and allow themselves the fullest expression of their respective and highly individual sexualities, which, in the final analysis, is really the greatest strength, not only of human beings, but of most living things.

So the question invariably arises: how can we express our *true selves*? According to Bruce Lee, the answer is, first of all, to get rid of the ego, or excessive self-consciousness. A certain "spiritual loosening" is required, and this can be obtained only when one masters the principle of what the Chinese call *wu-hsin* (the Japanese, *mushin*), literally "no-mind," or the deregulation of self-consciousness.

The Way of No-Mindedness

The concept of wu-hsin does not mean an empty mind that is devoid of all emotion, nor is it simply quietness of mind. As Bruce Lee explained the concept:

Although quietude and calmness are necessary, it is the "nongraspingness" of the mind that mainly constitutes the principle of "no-mindedness." A gung fu man employs his mind as a mirror—it grasps nothing, yet it refuses nothing; it receives, but does not keep. As Alan Watts put it, no-mindedness is a "state of wholeness in which the mind functions freely and easily, without the sensation of a second mind or ego standing over it with a club."[2] What he means is to let the mind think what it likes without the interference by the separate thinker or ego within oneself. So long as it thinks what it wants, there is absolutely no effort in letting go, and the disappearance of the effort to let go is precisely the disappearance of the separate thinker.

Still, to some of us, the question surfaces: but how do we "let go"? Bruce Lee responded:

There is nothing to try to do, for whatever comes up moment by moment is accepted, including nonacceptance. No-mindedness is then not being without emotion or feeling, but being one in whom feeling is not sticky or blocked. It is a mind immune to emotional influences, like a river in which everything is flowing on ceaselessly without cessation or standing still.

In other words, wu-hsin is a process of employing the mind to see the totality, and not the segments; it is looking at the whole tree, in all of its glory, as opposed to the individual leaf. According to Chuang-tzu, the disciple of Lao-tzu:

The baby looks at things all day without winking,
That is because his eyes are not focused on any particular object.
He goes without knowing where he is going,
And stops without knowing what he is doing.
He merges himself with the surroundings
And moves along with it—these are the principles of mental hygiene.[3]

In other words, concentration should not have the usual sense of restricting the attention to a single sense object; rather, it is simply a quiet awareness of whatever happens to be here and now. The condition of no-mindedness allows one's mind to be present everywhere because it is present nowhere. According to Bruce Lee:

> *A gung fu man's mind . . . can remain present because even when related to this or that object, it does not cling to it. The flow of thought is like water filling a pond, which is always ready to flow off again. It can work its inexhaustible power because it is free, and be open to everything because it is empty.*

This phenomena of wu-hsin has many other names—even within the Chinese language. Phrases such as *pen hsin* (original mind), *hsin hsin* (faith in mind), and *fu hsin* (Buddha mind) are all variants of wu-hsin, or the non-segmented totality of our complete psychic faculty. Bruce Lee made the observation that any arresting of our conscious awareness on only one thought, aspect, subject, object, or focal point created a condition of "psychical stoppage"—the antithesis of wu-hsin. Such a segmented thought process, Lee believed, leads to a condition of hesitation or detachment from the *now* and thereby creates the potential for serious problems—particularly for those confronted with a life-or-death situation (see Alan Watts's essay "The Tao of Wu-hsin" in the appendix of this book). As Lee noted:

> *The basic problem of a martial artist is known as psychical stoppage. When he is engaged in a deadly contest with his antagonist, his mind often attaches itself to thoughts or any object it encounters. Unlike the fluid mind in everyday life, his mind is "stopped," incapable of flowing from one object to another without stickiness or clogginess. He ceases to be master of himself, and as a result, his tools no longer express themselves in their suchness. So to have something in one's mind means that it is preoccupied and has no time for anything else; however, to attempt to remove the thought already in it is to refill it with another something!*

In other words, thinking about achieving a state of nonfixatedness, or no-mindedness, entails an application of mental effort, or what the Chinese call *wei* (unnatural striving), which effectively prevents its attainment. It is the equivalent of trying to relax by saying "I must relax!" the fallacy of which was pointed out by Lee in Chapter 5. In order to achieve this natural state of nonanalytical observance and comprehension, a mental state of purposeless must be present, of which Lee had this to say:

> *Ultimately one should be "purposeless." By purposeless is not meant the mere absence of things where vacant nothingness prevails. The object is not to be stuck with thought process. The spirit is by nature formless, and no "objects" are to be stuck in it. When anything is stuck there, your psychic energy loses its balance, its native activity becomes cramped and no longer flows with the stream. . . . But when there prevails a state of purposelessness (which is also a state of fluidity, empty-mindedness, or simply the everyday mind), the spirit harbors nothing in it, nor is it tipped in any one direction; it transcends both subject and object; it responds empty-mindedly to environmental changes and leaves no track.*

A Feline Analogy

This quality of not being "tipped in any one direction," of not clinging to things or being off center, is observed quite readily in the behavior of most animals, and particularly in cats. When a cat leaps from the top of a table, for example, the cat simply lets go of itself; it becomes completely relaxed and lands on the ground with a gentle thud and continues on its way. The cat does not fill its mind with all sorts of thoughts as to how it shall land, where it shall go once it does, or—least of all—whether it is "safe" to make the leap in the first place.

To follow through with our illustration, if that same cat, in the midst of leaping from the table, decided that it did not want to leap at all, it would instantly become tense in trying to change its course and would end up in a rather sorry state once it hit the ground. And so in the same way, wu-hsin is the avoidance of such mental tenseness, of *paralysis by analysis.*

In this respect, the philosophy of wu-hsin, or no-mindedness, as espoused by Bruce Lee can be likened to the natural response of the cat leaping from the tabletop. That is to say, the moment we are born, we can be said to be, metaphorically speaking, placed in a state of hurdling from a position of *existence*—in which we are secure in our surroundings—to one of *nonexistence* (in which we are not). We are, in effect, in a state of "falling" toward death, and there's nothing that can stop us. Granted, some of us are given a greater height to fall from, which prolongs our descent somewhat, but we are all falling nonetheless. However, instead of our going into a state of tension at the thought of this fact and attempting to mentally cling to all sorts of things during our descent (such as our memories of the past or hopes for the future, which have no existence in our immediate reality), we should endeavor to be more catlike in our perspective on life. This is a perspective that is perhaps best illustrated in this Zen poem:

> While living, be a dead man.
> Thoroughly dead.
> And then whatever you do,
> just as you will, will be right.[4]

In other words, attempting to arrest your fall (reality) by attaching yourself to objects that are themselves impermanent will, ultimately, yield you nothing. It must be remembered that there is nothing that does not change (move) in order to be permanent (to live)—which in itself is a Yin/Yang statement. It is also a case of the law of inversion, or what the great Zen teacher Alan Watts called the law of paradox. That is to say, in one sense, the more *dead* you become, the more *alive* you become. The more soft you become, the stronger you become.

This, in essence, is the principle of "bend and survive," and it's perfectly illustrated by Bruce Lee's image of the two trees with which we began this chapter. In the snow, the trunk of the firm tree stands rigid, and as the snow piles up and up, the branch doesn't give an inch—until finally it snaps under the weight of its burden. The willow, however, bends instantly when even a little bit of snow accumulates on its branch, thereby effectively removing the burden of the snow and allowing the branch to spring back up again, fresh and renewed. This is not, then, a case of weakness or limpness. It is not softness in the sense of being just limp and flaccid, but of being springy, of having give. Thus, the willow's example reveals to us that we can only achieve what we want to achieve through a process of yielding with adversity—of letting go. This, after all, is the easiest possible course and, some might observe, the very height of intelligence. As Lee once wrote:

> *Nothingness cannot be confined;*
> *Gentleness cannot be snapped.*

And so the question is posed, what type of person are you? Do you choose to be the strong, stoic type—like the firm tree—who allows personal problems to pile up one upon the other until you, too, snap? Or are you more like the willow: one who does not resist the weight of problematic burden, or who endures it but rather gently bends by dealing with each problem as it presents itself so that you can spring back stronger than before and, by so yielding, live a life that is free of compound emotional turmoil? Bruce Lee was the latter type of person, and he taught his students that the best way to tackle adversity was first to learn to yield to it:

> *A good JKD does not oppose force or give way completely. He is pliable as a spring; he is the complement and not the opposition of his opponent's strength. HE HAS NOT TECHNIQUE; HE MAKES HIS OPPONENT'S TECHNIQUE HIS TECHNIQUE. He has no design; he makes opportunity his design.*

To attain a state of wu-hsin, however, requires a special type of action, or rather, a special type of nonaction, that is known in Chinese as *wu-wei*, and in Japanese as *mui*.

Nonaction

The principle of wu-wei (literally, "nonstriving") indicates that harmony—either within or without—cannot be obtained by going against the grain of things, which only promotes conflicts and extreme reaction. When one allows one's self-consciousness, or ego, to yield to the natural flow of things, the highest action is obtained—the action of no action. Bruce Lee described the process thusly:

> Wu *means "not" or "non," and* wei *means "action," "doing," "striving," "straining," or "busying." However, it doesn't really mean doing nothing, but to let one's mind alone, trusting it to work by itself. The most important thing is not to strain in any way. Wu-wei, in gung fu, means spirit or mind action, in the sense that the governing force is the mind and not that of the senses. During sparring, a gung fu man learns to forget about himself and follows the movement of his opponent, leaving his mind free to make its own counter-movement without any resistance, and adopts a supple attitude. His actions are all performed without self-assertion; he lets his mind remain spontaneous and ungrasped. As soon as he stops to think, his flow of movement will be disturbed, and he is immediately struck by his opponent. Every action, therefore, has to be done "unintentionally" without ever trying.*

Such unintentional, effortless action was a trademark of Bruce Lee's. Watching Lee in action, you note that the one central, fundamental thing in his technique is that he responds to any attack without interval. This principle is also observable in dancing (in which Lee was also well versed, having won the cha-cha championship of the Crown Colonies in 1958). Good dancing partners typically move as if they are but one single organism; there is no interval between the man's lead and the woman's following. When a man is accustomed to a partner with whom he's worked for some time, she almost feels to him as if she were part of his body because she moves so completely responsively to his initiative.

In much the same way, the leaf on the bough of a tree responds to the initiative of the wind; the wind blows and the leaf simply goes along with it. The same is true when you see a ball floating upon the water. It responds instantly to the slightest modulation of the waves. And this attitude of there *being no interval* is the real meaning, to Bruce Lee's way of thinking, of wu-wei. It entails a high degree of mental or spiritual balance, of not being tipped in any one direction or inclining toward extremes of any nature. This attitude of being emotionally and spiritually centered, or in balance, is one of the core tenets of Bruce Lee's philosophy and, indeed, the fundamental precept of Yin/Yang.

The Role of Balance

Balance is one of the primary—almost axiomatic—concepts of Taoist philosophy as the philosophy of the Tao has a basic respect for the natural balance inherent in all things. In the realm of nature, for example, you wouldn't volitionally opt to upset this balance; rather, you would try to adapt yourself to its flow. In other words, you should always try to go along with it and avoid, say, the kind of mistake made in the 1950s by the World Health Organization (WHO). In its attempt to eliminate malaria in northern Borneo, WHO employed the pesticide dieldrin on the local mosquito population, which was known to carry the disease. At first, the people at WHO believed they had solved the problem, since the use of the chemical had significantly diminished the abundance of mosquitoes (and even flies and cockroaches) and, along with them, the incidence of malaria. But then a strange thing happened: the roofs of the villagers' huts began to collapse on top of them and a typhoid epidemic broke out.

The reason was that local lizards began eating the insects that were laden with the dieldrin. The lizards, full of the toxic chemical, were eaten by the cats of the village, and that effectively wiped out the cat population. With the cats gone, the local rat population skyrocketed, and they ran unchecked throughout the villages, carrying with them typhus-infested fleas. The roofs then began collapsing because the dieldrin, in addition to killing the mosquitoes, cockroaches, and flies, also killed the wasps that ordinarily would have consumed the caterpillars that, left unchecked, were now eating the villagers' thatched roofs. Through such an interference with the balance of nature, the WHO, for a time, found itself in some difficulty.

The philosophy of balance, or rather the respect for balance, is perhaps best illustrated by squeezing a rubber ball. However or wherever you squeeze it, the ball will yield, but it never loses its balance. It's the safest form in the world, completely contained and never off center. To be completely contained, never susceptible to being put off center or phased by anything, is what is aimed at in the philosophy of Bruce Lee.

Similarly, those of us who wish to cultivate a stress-free existence have to be possessed of this same sense of balance, never being put off center no matter how hard we seem to get squeezed. We have to learn how to flow with life in the same way that the ball responds to the movements of the water, that the leaf travels with the wind, and that the martial artist cultivates a state of harmony between himself and his opponent. When we can accomplish this, we need never again be snared by conflict—of any kind.

CHAPTER SEVEN

RELATIONSHIPS

Life is a constant process of relating. Man is living in a relationship, and in relationships we grow.

BRUCE LEE

∞

Bruce Lee's philosophy makes the point that we are part of a vast universal process and that it is impossible for human beings to live in a vacuum or to be isolated. In other words, to exist is to be related—in some capacity. Lee defined relationship as an interconnected challenge and response between two entities, whether between husband and wife, parent and child, individual and individual (in the sense of nonintimate relations), nation and nation, or life and death—and any corollary of these primary relationships. The relationship of individual to individual, in fact, is what gives rise to the corollary concept of *society*, as the compounding of individuals is what creates the mass, or group, that collectively is known as society.

Similarly, the concept of family is a corollary of the relationships of husband and wife, and parent and child, which, in turn, form the relationship of intimacy, or communion. To communicate with one another, then, is obviously a form of relationship. Relationship—the concept—is, in fact, a process of self-revelation, and self-revelation is simply the offspring born of observing oneself in relationship with others.

Bruce and Linda Lee were the textbook example of a relationship that was perfectly centered in the principle of Yin/Yang.

Undoubtedly, countless forms of relationships exist within our universe (and indeed, as we have seen, within our very bodies), and to address them all is quite beyond the scope of this book. We shall nevertheless focus on the five primary relationships we have just touched upon.

Husband and Wife

In the case of the relationship of husband and wife, Bruce Lee's marriage to Linda was a perfect symbiosis of two independent though interconnected halves that would, in time, merge into one greater totality. In many respects, their relationship was a perfect example of Yin/Yang, with Lee's personality serving often as pure Yang, in the sense of being extroverted, masculine, and forceful, and his wife Linda being the perfect complementary component to these qualities in the form of pure Yin, being more introverted, feminine, and flexible.

Together, they complemented and completed the totality of the other; when one would expand, the other would contract, and vice versa. For example, when Bruce, who had been the principle breadwinner of the family, was unable to work owing to a severe back injury he sustained in early 1970, Linda instantly filled the gap by taking an evening job. When Linda was down about something, Bruce was up, with the result that his positiveness raised her spirits to a point more closely approximating perfect balance. Their energies flowed together and adapted—like water—to whatever obstacles appeared in their path. By so doing, husband and wife were able to successfully navigate—and thus pass safely through—all manner of adversity.

Bruce Lee, in an interview in the early 1960s commented on the philosophic aspects of his relationship with his wife: *"Linda and I aren't one and one. We are two halves that make a whole. You have to apply yourself to be a family—two halves fitted together are more efficient than either half would ever be alone."*

In what little spare time he could find, Lee was fond of translating Chinese poetry into English. One such poem, by the ancient Chinese poet Tzu Yeh, contained a stanza that underscored perfectly Lee's beliefs regarding the relationship of husband and wife:

> Do you not see
> That you and I
> Are as the branches
> Of one tree?
> With your rejoicing
> Comes my laughter;
> With your sadness
> Start my tears.
> Love,
> Could life be otherwise,
> With you and me?

When one reads these lines, one immediately recalls Lee's words from Chapter 4 regarding the wholeness and coexistence of all things and the nature of complementaries. One truly could not survive but for the existence of the other, and this is never more apparent than in relationships in which love is a part.

Love—as Relationship

The nature of love, according to Bruce Lee, is one of the more difficult concepts to comprehend. It is not obtained by intellectual urgency; it cannot be created by strict adherence to various doctrines, which only render the term sterile and empty. As Bruce Lee put it: *"If one loves, one need not have an ideology of love."*

Instead, love—true love, that is—is a state or condition of *being* wherein the activities of the self have ceased. I say "ceased"—as opposed to their simply being suppressed or denied. To experience this state, an understanding of the workings of the self in all of its many varieties of consciousness is required. It can be said that there is a true relationship only when love is present, but what do we mean by love? Perhaps we can understand this state better by first understanding what love is not.

First off, to what I'm sure will be the chagrin of many, love is *not* sex. Although having said that, sex is indeed, a part of love. In other words, there is definitely a physical component to the experience of love, an involvement of the body as well as of the mind, and it is a mutual experience. That is to say, you must believe, on one level, that there is something constant about the body or the physical appearance of the person with whom you are experiencing this sensation of love and that this physical constant is inherently and intrinsically enduring and tightly "connected" to what you perceive to be the identity of the person in question. Were it otherwise, if the body of the individual in question were perceived as impermanent (which, in reality, it truly is), you would in effect be "in love" with, by definition, a *different person* every day.

As we've seen, however, we *do* change or perhaps it would be more accurate to say that we are change, as it is our very ability to change with change that Bruce Lee referred to as being "the changeless state." The key to success in love is to have its experience transcend your physical body (and the subatomic variations that comprise it), in order for the love to evolve in symbiosis with the pure essence of the other individual with whom you are experiencing this powerful emotional state. Inasmuch as you are successful in this regard, the sensation of love will endure. Where simultaneous evolution of the spirit or, in this case, the emotion of love is not present, a state of not being able to *change with change* results in a *changed* state—with the result that two lovers eventually and quite literally "grow apart."

What often happens when two individuals cling solely to the physical component of their relationship is that they sooner or later (and mostly sooner) end up frustrated. They have to, as this is the natural result of trying to cling to—or possess—nature itself. If you don't cling to it but rather let it evolve in its own natural process, you can have a truly wonderful experience. But the attempt to possess another individual goes against the grain of Tao. Think about this for a moment; the person who possesses is in effect saying, "I love you so much that *I must own you*," thereby preventing the other person—and the relationship itself—from living, evolving, and growing. This dooms the relationship to the very opposite of growth: death.

Please don't mistake this perspective as being antirelationship or antimarriage, because it is, in fact, just the opposite. However, it must be stressed—in the strongest possible terms—that possessiveness is the opposite of love. It is, indeed, the projection of an individual ego over the soul of another, much like the humorous story of the man who claimed: "I loved my wife so much that I climbed a mountain and named it after her—I called it Mount *Mrs. Jimmy Kindela!*" Oh! Be still my heart!

If you try to possess people and you make your sexual passion possessive in any way, then you are, in effect, trying to cling to the physical world. Since the physical world is itself illusory, you're engaging in nonreality-based behavior, and this will doom your relationships to failure. If, however, your experience of love can allow you to "let go" by not clinging or attempting to possess another, you'll find your relationships will not only become far more interesting, but will grow into a very strong unity of body, mind, and spirit. In other words, love can only exist in an environment that is free of ego—where one has forgotten oneself.

To Bruce Lee, one did not have or possess "love" but rather lived the emotion in the present to the fullest possible degree and reveled in the experience of it. Lee was of the opinion that the love and happiness he enjoyed with his wife was built upon their ability not to "be in love" but simply to "love." This tremendous physical, mental, and spiritual experience, according to Lee, grew most successfully out of a solid base of friendship. In what remains one of the most lyrical definitions ever given on the subject, Lee described love thusly: *"Love is like a friendship caught on fire. In the beginning, a flame, very pretty, often hot and fierce, but still only light and flickering. As love grows older, our hearts mature and our love becomes as coals, deep burning and unquenchable."*

The happiness that a couple enjoys should be derived, Bruce Lee believed, not from a whirlwind romance that involves an extreme emotional state, but from a more balanced relationship (remember that true Yin/Yang is expressed through temperance and moderation—not by running to extremes). Lee once noted:

> *The happiness that is derived from excitement is like a brilliant fire—soon it will go out. Before we married, we never had the chance to go out to night-clubs. We only spent our nights watching TV and chatting. Many young couples live a very exciting life when they are in love. So, when they marry, and their lives are reduced to calmness and dullness, they will feel impatient and will drink the bitter cup of a sad marriage.*

Yin/Yang and Midlife Changes

Lee's point is well taken. In a previous chapter, we learned about the problems inherent in attempting to defy the natural order or balance of things. And this point is perhaps never more true than in the subject of relationships. Many of us have heard of the concept of *male menopause*: that time in life (believed to be around age forty) when a man looks back on his life and suddenly panics, thinking that life (read: *living*) has almost passed him by. At such a stage, the male of our species will engage in all manner of pathetic ploys (from buying a toupee, to speeding around in a new sportscar, to chasing younger women) in an attempt to "turn back the clock," to a time when he actually "lived life" or, at least, "had some fun" out of it.

The reason for this skewed perspective—if in fact male menopause truly exists—is that nothing endures in excess and, going through life from the outside looking in (i.e., the Western mode of hyperanalysis) will result in the suppression of actually living life for the purpose of analyzing it. One can stand on the sidelines, suppressing reality, for only so long before snapping and rebounding to the extreme opposite direction. You may recall Bruce Lee's words from Chapter 3: *"Living exists when life lives* THROUGH *us—unhampered in its flow, for he who is living is not conscious of living, and in this is the life* IT *lives."*

Lee taught that we must be aware of the interrelatedness of microcosm and macrocosm, that we must come to understand our unity with nature and with one another. Lee also held that the way to allow life to live through us is not by standing apart from it and analyzing it (the Western approach), but through relaxing and letting life flow through us, understanding that we are all part of the vast cosmic cycles of energetic flow as embodied in the principle of balance within Yin/Yang: *"Nothing can be secured by extremes. . . . Only sober moderation lasts, and that persists through all time. Only the midpart of anything is preserved because the pendulum [of life] must have balance, and the midpart is the balance."*

It is easy to see how a lifetime spent in working nine to five, of thinking analytically about paying the bills, meeting the mortgage, earning that bonus, and planning for retirement can lead to one's feeling as though life has, indeed, passed one by—whether it occurs at age forty or later. The key, then, to getting the most out of life lies simply in your decision to live your life in accordance with the principle of Yin/Yang and to learn to cooperate with—as opposed to standing apart from—the natural patterns of our world. This is precisely what Bruce Lee meant when he said: *"I couldn't live by a rigid schedule. I try to live freely from moment to moment letting things happen and adjusting to them."*

In other words, simply let your career and daily activities be harmonious expressions of who you truly are.

Parent and Child

On the topic of parent-child relationships, Bruce Lee thought it important to instill a strong sense of "family" in his children. According to Lee:

> *It may not be as easy to develop that attitude [of respect for one's family] in the United States as it is in Hong Kong. That's one reason why I would like for my children to go to school in Hong Kong for a while, so they can better learn to respect their family and its traditions—and that way gain self-respect.*

Bruce Lee's proudest moments were unquestionably the births of his two children. Here, proud father Bruce shares a moment with daughter Shannon (left) and son Brandon.

Bruce Lee observed that in the Orient, because of the strong sense of family relationship, there wasn't the same degree of delinquency or disrespect that existed among many of the youngsters in North America. He noted: *"Hong Kong is a British colony, you know, and is about half Western. Even so, a Chinese boy growing up there knows that if he disgraces himself, he brings disgrace upon all his kin—upon a great circle of people. And I think this is good."*

Lee noted during his formative years in Hong Kong that the standard child-rearing belief of the elder Chinese families was that a son could never—never—contradict his parents. While he found much to admire about this method, he was nevertheless glad that the passage of time and the influence of the West had made this once unimpeachable rule more of a guideline in most of today's Hong Kong households. He pointed out: *"My father never struck me, and I'm not planning to strike Brandon. I think a father can control the situation by swinging with it. You know what I mean?"*

Indeed! Wasn't "swinging with it" the very advice given to a young Bruce Lee from his gung fu instructor, Yip Man? Wasn't this proven to be the way closest resembling nature's own in dealing with adversity? It is, after all, simply the application of Yin to a problem of Yang. If a stubborn child is behaving in a Yang capacity (obstinate, forceful, etc.), you would accomplish nothing by meeting this Yang force with additional Yang force (i.e., in the form of arguing with or striking the child). The principle of noninterference with nature would indicate that we must allow our children's natural personalities to develop and find expression. However, if their personalities become forceful or in any way disruptive to the natural pattern of Tao, then the only solution would be the natural one: complementing their Yang behavior with an equal proportion of Yin.

In a passage from the *Tao te ching* that was directed toward those that sought to govern (whether a state, a department, or a family), Lao-tzu made the following observation:

—30—

Whoever relies on Tao in governing men
doesn't try to force issues
or defeat enemies by force of arms.
For every force there is a counterforce.
Violence, even well intentioned,
always rebounds upon oneself.

The Master does his job
and then stops.
He understands that the universe is forever out of control,
and that trying to dominate events
goes against the current of the Tao.[1]

The result being that the child will now have their imbalanced and inappropriate Yang energy centered and channeled into a more manageable, moderate, and desirable (from a parental point of view!) mode of behavior.

Shortly after the birth of his son, Brandon, in 1965, Lee was asked what lessons he, as a new father, hoped to impart to his son. His answer bears consideration from all parents and parents-to-be:

Brandon is being brought up in the midst of two cultures. There are good points in Chinese culture; there are good points in Occidental culture. He will take some principles from one, some from the other. Brandon will learn that Oriental culture and Occidental culture are not mutually exclusive, but mutually dependent. Neither would be remarkable if it were not for the existence of the other. Much of what Brandon will learn from Occidental culture, he will acquire, first from his mother, then from his childhood playmates, then from schooling.

Much of what Brandon will learn from Oriental culture will come from me, and I will have learned it from gung fu, in which the Zen influence is strong. Zen has derived many of its concepts from the Chinese belief in balance: Yin, which is feminine and gentle, and Yang, which is masculine and firm. Having accepted that basic idea, another must be added: there is no such thing as pure Yin or pure Yang. Gentleness should cloak firmness; firmness should be modified by gentleness. No woman should follow passively. She must learn that there is an active way of following. She must have what the Occidentals call "backbone." By the same reasoning, no man should be totally firm; his resolve must be softened by compassion.

Once Brandon has learned to understand Yin and Yang, he will know that nothing can be secured by extremes. For instance, the haircuts worn by many boys at this time are not haircuts at all, but disguises. The fashion cannot last, because it is extreme and will soon tire the wearer and the beholder. Possibly the beholder more quickly, but a vast boredom for all in any case. Only sober moderation lasts, and that persists through all time. Only the midpart of anything is preserved because the pendulum must have balance, and the midpart is the balance.

There is another bit of Chinese philosophy that has a bearing on problems common to all humankind. We say: "The oak tree is mighty, yet it will be destroyed by a mighty wind because it resists the elements; the bamboo bends with the wind, and by bending, survives." We advance the idea by saying: "Be pliable. When a man is living, he is soft and pliable; when he is dead, he becomes rigid." Pliability is life; rigidity is death, whether one speaks of one's own prejudices or actions. Further, one should not try to hyperanalyze one's life, and to try to evaluate it.

To stand on the outside and try to look inside is futile; whatever was there will go away. This also applies to a nebulous thing described as "happiness." To try to identify it is like turning on a light to look at darkness. Analyze it, and it is gone.

We have a Zen parable that tells of a man who said, "Master, I must seek liberation."

The teacher asked, "And who binds you?"

The student answered, "I do not know. Perhaps I bind myself."

So the teacher said, "In that case, why seek liberation of me? In summer we sweat; in winter we shiver."

So the student thought, "He is speaking of a secret place where our only problem is the seasons of the year."

I will teach Brandon that each man binds himself; the fetters are ignorance, laziness, preoccupation with self, and fear. He must liberate himself, while accepting the fact that we are of this world, so that "in summer we sweat; in winter we shiver."

Individual and Individual

Marsha was the office gossip. She always knew "the latest" about so-and-so. She lived vicariously through the lives and deeds of others; as long as someone—somewhere—was doing something that might be of interest—to someone—Marsha felt that by her reporting it, her life had meaning.

Whenever you encounter such a person as Marsha, she is to be pitied. She is, spiritually speaking, lost. Her journey along the path toward finding her true self has somehow been preempted—only she hasn't realized it. Marsha has ended up under the illusion that her identity is connected to her ability to please others by being able to "get the story" of somebody else's private affairs.

However, as the Tao clearly points out, this is not the way to get people to accept you:

—30—

Because he believes in himself,
he doesn't try to convince others.
Because he is content with himself,
he doesn't need others' approval.
Because he accepts himself,
the whole world accepts him.[2]

This may bring to mind images of our friend Jeff from Chapter 2, and like Jeff, the Marshas of the world never experience peace of mind or feelings of true fulfillment in their endeavors. The reason is that in order to make a critical report on another person's life or, more peculiarly, on another person's motivation or character, first requires one to stand apart from one's own life for the purpose of analyzing and criticizing another's. This, to Bruce Lee's way of thinking, was simply a case of looking in the wrong direction—especially if peace of mind, born of self-understanding, was the objective:

> Yes, we possess a pair of eyes, the function of which is to observe, to discover, etc. Yet many of us simply do not really see in the true sense of the word. I must say that when the eyes are used externally to observe the inevitable faults of other beings, most of us are rather quick with readily equipped condemnation. For it is easy to criticize and break down the spirit of others, but to know yourself takes maybe a lifetime. To take responsibility of one's actions, good and bad, is something else. After all, knowledge simply means self-knowledge.

People like Marsha never enjoy their own life in its suchness because they're no longer open to it. They've blocked the inner spiritual channels through which life flows. If they're fortunate, somewhere along their journey the dense gray fog will lift and they'll be able to get back on track by somehow "emptying their cup" and taking in a healthier, more positive, and personally edifying perspective. If they're unfortunate, they'll instead become successful through being rewarded by others for the suppression of their spirit (whether by receiving a salaried raise from an equally insecure boss who "wants to know what his employees are doing" or by making a profession of their habit of external analysis by becoming, say, professional "gossip" reporters).

You might note an apparent conflict here: as long as one is well paid or successful, how can this be an unfortunate thing? It is an unfortunate occurrence in as much as it serves as an incentive to the Marshas of the world to remain within their spiritual trance, to call off their inner search and continue on as an observer from the sidelines of life, never knowing what it would have been like to ever *take part* in the game. It is, in effect, a death sentence for the soul. The inner warrior of a woman like Marsha shall never reach full expression, thereby eclipsing even the possibility of her ever knowing reality or truth, and preventing the attainment of inner peace and a contented lifestyle.

The most interesting people we can encounter are, by and large, the ones who are the *doers* of deeds, not the chroniclers. The doers *live* life, sampling liberally the various colors upon its vast palette, and experience the full emotional spectrum of joy, sadness, pleasure, and pain. The doers learn how to adapt themselves to life's vicissitudes as the cork adapts itself to the modulations of the waves. As Bruce Lee pointed out, there is so much to learn about *you*—about your innermost self—that spending your time in analyzing the behavior of others is time that is irretrievably lost, like grains of sand from life's hourglass. Time that should have been spent in the greater, far more rewarding search for your higher self.

Nation shall speak to nation: with **Enter the Dragon (1973),** *the first-ever coproduction between Chinese and American filmmakers, Lee felt that he had brought the East a little closer to the West. Here, he and American costar John Saxon flash the peace sign for the camera.*

Nation and Nation

Bruce Lee was hopeful that through his films he could accomplish two things: one, reveal the Chinese culture in a dignified and educational way to Western audiences, and two, educate the masses of the East to some of the more sophisticated elements of Western culture, such as art and film-making. As nations are composed of people, the issue of relationships as they pertain to nations is one of relating to large masses of people. As to the issue of "fear thy neighbor," Lee did not subscribe to it. When asked by a journalist in the late 1960s about Communist China's apparent hostility toward the West, Lee replied: *"Like any poor country or person they are hostile while they are down. If you have nothing, you can afford to be hostile. But wait until they, too, become more prosperous. They will soon quiet down and want peace just like the rest of the world."*

He was particularly optimistic about the possibilities that could develop by the East and West getting together. When asked his thoughts on what President Richard Nixon's visit to China in the early 1970s meant with regard to the potential benefits to both cultures, he responded: *"Once the opening of China happens, it will bring more understanding! More things that to the Western eye will seem different, you know? And maybe in the contrast of comparison, some new thing might grow. So, therefore, it's a very rich period to be in."*

Ironically, while Lee's perspective on East/West relations was very philosophical, Lee himself would have disagreed vehemently with Plato on the subject of politics, for he considered the worst conceivable government would be one that was run by philosophers. They botch every natural process with theory, and their ability to make speeches and multiply ideas is precisely the sign of their incapacity for action. As Bruce Lee said:

Knowing is not enough; we must apply.
Willing is not enough; we must do.

The Western philosopher or intellectual could actually be considered a danger to his society because he constantly thinks in terms of rules and laws; he wishes to construct a society like geometry and does not realize that such regulation destroys the living freedom and vitality of the parts. In following the Taoist ideals of nonanalysis, the ideal leader or ruler would be one who regulated his subjects as little as possible; if he guided the nation, it would be away from all artifice and complexity toward a state of artless simplicity, in which life would follow the wisely thoughtless routine of nature.

What is nature's "routine"? In a phrase, it is a routine of *nonroutine*. Nature is natural activity, the silent flow of traditional events, the majestic order of the seasons and the sky; it is the Tao, or Way, exemplified and embodied in every brook and rock and star; it is that impartial, impersonal, and yet rational law of things to which the law of conduct must conform if human beings truly desire to live in wisdom and peace. This law of things is, as we have seen, the Tao of the universe, just as the law of conduct is the Way of life; in truth, thought Bruce Lee, both Tao's are one, and human life, in its essential and wholesome rhythm, is part of the universal rhythm of the world.

The closest philosophical perspective to this in the Western world was the hypothesis of The Absolute as set forth by Georg Wilhelm Friedrich Hegel (1770–1831). The Absolute was taken to be the sum total of all things in their development. Hegel postulated God as Reason and Reason as the web and structure of natural law within which life or spirit grows and evolves. This concept was actually anticipated in the West by Baruch Spinoza (1632–1677) with his notion that all of reality is but a single substance, which he called *"Deus sive Natura"* (God or Nature), a form, if you will, of the cosmic Tao. According to Bruce Lee's philosophy, it is in a similar cosmic Tao that all the laws of nature are united to create an almost Spinozian substance of all reality. In it, all natural forms and varieties find their proper place, and all apparent diversities and contradictions meet; it is The Absolute in which all particulars are resolved into one vast and interdependent web of Hegelian unity.

Life and Death

In the grand scheme of relationships, there is none so inevitable—nor so close—as life and death. These complementaries are the extreme antipodes of Yin/Yang, which means that a hair's breadth separates them. Growing old and death are the way of things, the natural way. Any passing prior to old age is tragedy, a flower cut off prior to its blossoming. Barring accident, death is reserved for the aged, with the result that youth and death meet one another as they walk the streets. Indeed, life feeds upon death, life's endurance being predicated on the perpetual birth and death of individual cells.

Shortly before this book went to press my father died. He was eighty-five and died, technically, of "old age." It caused me to pause for a moment to consider just what exactly old age is, in its relationship to the life cycle. It struck me, as indeed it must have Bruce Lee, that once we understand the nature of this relationship (and again, it's yet another example of Yin/Yang), we find that we have less cause for grief. According to Will Durant, who, incidentally, was a favorite philosopher of my father's:

Fundamentally, old age is a condition of the flesh, of protoplasm that finds inevitably the limit of its life. It is a hardening of the arteries and categories, a retardation of thought and blood; a man is as old as his arteries and as young as his ideas.

The ability to learn decreases with each decade of our lives, as if the association fibers of the brain were accumulated and overlaid in inflexible patterns. New material seems no longer to find room, and recent impressions fade as rapidly as a politician's promises—and the public's memory. As decay proceeds, threads and unities are lost, and coordination wavers; the old man falls into a digressive circumstantiality.

Then, just as the child grew more rapidly the younger it was, so the old man ages more quickly with every day. And just as the child was protected by insensitivity on its entry into the world, so old age is eased by an apathy of sense and will, as nature slowly administers a general anesthesia before she permits time's scythe to complete the most major of operations. . . . As sensations diminish in intensity, the sense of vitality fades; the desire for life gives way to indifference and patient waiting; the fear of death is strangely mingled with the longing for repose. Perhaps then, if one has lived well, if one has known the full term of love and all the juice and ripeness of experience, one can die with some measure of content."[3]

So spoke Will Durant of old age in 1929. Bruce Lee, in a script that he collaborated on with Stirling Silliphant and James Coburn, had the protagonist of the story, a martial artist named Cord, meet the embodiment of death as one of three trials that he had to pass en route to self-mastery. During the moments preceding their encounter, Cord speaks to himself of acceptance and an almost Durantian "apathy" toward death:

Of course you're there. Death is always there. So why was I afraid? Your leap is swift. You claws are sharp and merciful. What can you take from me which is not already yours? . . . Everything I have done until now has been fruitless. It has led to nothing. There was no other path except that it led to nothing—and before me now there is only one real fact—Death. The truth I have been seeking—this truth is Death. Yet Death is also a seeker. Forever seeking me. So—we have met at last. And I am prepared. I am at peace. Because I will conquer death with death.

In other words, by dying to the desire to cling to life for fear of death, we are liberated from the fear of death. That is to say, if you can obtain a mental state of accepting that you have nothing tethering you to this earth or this life, then you've got nothing to lose, for if you possess no attachments in this world, then there is nothing that would cause you to live in fear of losing them. Once this attitude has been accepted, you are then free to proceed forward in life with an unobstructed mind.

The German poet Johann Wolfgang Goethe (1749–1832) once wrote of this phenomenon in his poem *"Selige Sehnsucht"* ("Ecstasy and Desire") from the *West Ostlicher Divan*:

> Und solang du das nicht hast,
> Dieses: Stirb und werde!
> Bist du nur ein truber Gast
> Auf der dunklen Erde.

> (And so long as you do not have knowledge
> of this commandment: Die and become!
> You will be but a dismal guest on the dark earth.)[4]

As the Buddhist poem, written in China several centuries ago by Bunan, stated it:

"Youth and death meet each other as they walk the streets." Bruce Lee during the cemetery scene from **Enter the Dragon.**

> While living
> Be a dead man
> Be thoroughly dead—
> And behave as you like,
> And all's well.[5]

The result of such an understanding is a renunciation of the consciousness of self, or ego, and thereby a release of all things that would dam up the natural flow of things. Once this is out of the way, we are able to face life not only with a better understanding of its workings, but also with an ability to enjoy and respond to each life moment thereafter with renewed appreciation. In another script that Lee cowrote with Silliphant, Lee had his character say the following words:

Like everyone else, you want to learn the way to win, but never to accept the way to lose. To accept defeat—to learn to die—is to be liberated from it. Once you accept, you are free to flow and to harmonize. Fluidity is the way to an empty mind. So when tomorrow comes, you must free your ambitious mind and learn the art of dying.

By this, Lee was evoking the Taoist scripture of Lao-tzu, who wrote:

—16—

Empty your mind of all thoughts.
Let your heart be at peace.
Watch the turmoil of beings,
but contemplate their return.

Each separate being in the universe
returns to the common source.
Returning to the source is serenity.

If you don't realize the source,
you stumble in confusion and sorrow.
When you realize where you come from,
you naturally become tolerant,
disinterested, amused,
kindhearted as a grandmother,
dignified as a king.
Immersed in the wonder of the Tao,
you can deal with whatever life brings you,
and when death comes, you are ready.[1]

The fact that we must eventually cease to exist—that we will all eventually be claimed by what we call death—is not something to bemoan; it is, instead, the lot of our species and the fate of even the greatest of human beings. Titans such as Socrates, Lao-tzu, the Buddha, and Shakespeare—even Mr. Durant himself—eventually "shuffled off this mortal coil." No human being—however significant—escapes death's scythe. Lee noted this natural phenomenon during an interview in Hong Kong in 1972: *"Through the ages, the end for heroes is the same as ordinary men. They all died and gradually faded away in the memory of man. But when we are still alive, we have to understand ourselves, discover ourselves, and express ourselves. In this way, we can progress."*

In other words, at some point during the search to come to understand ourselves, we must accept the fact that existence in our present state of being must eventually cease. In fact, we've seen in earlier chapters that our physical selves are changing constantly and that our bodies are composed not of immutable solid matter but of energy. Further, we know that our energy is but an outcropping of truly infinite fields of energy that span the length and breadth of the universe. With this in mind, we again look to the words of Bruce Lee: *"To realize freedom, the mind has to learn to look at life, which is vast movement without the bondage of time, for freedom lies beyond the field of consciousness."*

This is certainly in agreement with Alan Watts, who said that we are indeed infinitely "more than a momentary flash of consciousness between two eternal darknesses." The fact that modern physics tells us we are composed not of matter but of infinite fields of energy suggests at least the possibility that the energy that is our life source is set free upon the expiration of our physical bodies. Certainly this would appear to have been Bruce Lee's belief: *"The soul of a man is an embryo in the body of man. The day of death is the day of wakening. The spirit lives on."*

Yet it remains hard for us to praise life when it abandons the ones we love. But this is largely due to an error in our perception of the life process, as Will Durant points out:

> *We are not individuals; and it is because we think ourselves such that death seems unforgivable. In reality, we are but temporary organs of our race, cells in the body of life; we die and drop away so that life may remain young and strong. If we were to live forever, growth would be stifled and youth would find no room on the earth. But through love we pass our vitality on to a new form of us before the old form dies; through parentage we bridge the chasm of the generations, and elude the enmity of death.*[7]

It is through progeny that our ancestors continue to live on—through their children and through their children's children. Posterity carries on the bloodlines, the appearance, and often the passions of those who are now no longer with us. So with some of you, death may indeed have claimed a victory over one you have loved dearly, but the reality of it is that it shall never win the war. Life always wins out through progeny as the cycle of Yin/Yang completes itself.

CHAPTER EIGHT

RACISM

*T*he belief that being born with a certain skin color or cultural heritage endows one with a moral superiority or rights of entitlement is a belief that should have died out with the notion of the divine right of kings.

Still, as evidenced with recent problems in Los Angeles and other major U.S. cities, the issue of racism is still very much with us in the twentieth century. The notion, however, that one has to be in a position of power in order to be a racist is inaccurate. Racism is born of the union of hatred and ignorance; it is a belief—not an entitlement—and therefore not the exclusive property of a particular social status. Racism is simply an incorrect perception of reality. Humans, regardless of color, are humans. Just as trees and flowers, no matter what their particular *species*, remain trees and flowers. The *genus*, or common root, of our humanity is the important thing, and this was the perspective of Bruce Lee.

As bad as racial relations may seem today, in the 1960s they were much worse. It is well established that both Bruce Lee and his wife, Linda, had to face some serious obstacles during the course of their relationship. Apart from the more common problems that most couples in society encounter, such as financial adversity, they had to overcome what in the 1960s was taboo in two cultures: an interracial marriage. However, in keeping with the philosophy they both shared, neither Bruce nor Linda allowed the perspective and prejudices of others—which they knew they were powerless to change—to affect the love they knew to exist and the incredibly unique relationship that they shared. According to Bruce Lee's philosophy, racist, prejudicial, or jingoistic beliefs were the result of not seeing the whole picture, of not understanding the universal underpinnings common to all races: *"Basically, human traits are the same everywhere. I don't want to sound like 'As Confucius says,' but under the sky, under the heavens, man, there is but one family. It just so happens that people are different."*

Lee, during an interview in Hong Kong in 1972, when asked to elaborate on his feelings regarding racial issues, revealed the following:

> *Although others may disagree, to me, racial barriers do not exist in reality. If I say that "everyone under the sun is a member of a universal family," you may think that I am bluffing and being idealistic. But if anyone still believes in racial differences, I think he is being too backward and narrow in his perspective. Perhaps he still does not understand man's equality and love.*

Will Durant echoed Lee's statements when he wove yet another of his brilliant word tapestries in his modest and poignant little book entitled *The Lessons of History*:

> "Racial" antipathies have some roots in ethnic origin, but they are also generated, perhaps predominantly, by differences of acquired culture— of language, dress, habits, morals, or religion. There is no cure for such antipathies except a broadened education. A knowledge of history may teach us that civilization is a co-operative product, that nearly all peoples have contributed to it; it is our common heritage and debt; and the civilized soul will reveal itself in treating every man or woman, however lowly, as a representative of one of these creative and contributory groups.[1]

Bruce Lee would have concurred with Durant on this point, for he believed that too many people were bound by the prejudices and traditions of their families, their communities, and their peers. If, for example, a parent tells a child that a particular race or group within a population is bad or evil, the child will typically grow up believing this is so. When, for example, the elder generation says no to something, then their children will strongly disapprove of it as well. As we saw in Chapter 3, however, life simply *is*—there are no *good* or *bad* forms of it. In fact, it is the very variety and multitudinous forms of life that make life interesting and a joy to experience. Nature plays no favorites, with the result that the red rose is not superior to the yellow rose—nor the rose to the carnation. They are simply as they are, always have been, and always will be.

It is a perspective that is beyond such classifications as good and evil, for and against, desirable and undesirable. As Watts once wrote:

> This is the sphere of the great universe. Looking out into it at night, we make no comparisons between right and wrong stars, nor between well and badly arranged constellations. Stars are by nature big and little, bright and dim. Yet the whole thing is a splendor and a marvel which sometimes makes our flesh creep with awe.[2]

And so it is with human beings, who, as you are certainly by now well aware, are as much a part of the universe as the stars Watts described. It is ignorance of this metaphysical fact that results in unchecked false premises—such as the belief in superior races—which are then handed down over generations until they become tradition. And it is always an uphill battle to unseat tradition from her throne, no matter how dishonestly she may hold sway over her subjects.

As we shall see in later chapters, tradition is also a huge impediment to the independent use of the mind in its quest to ascertain truth and serves to further impede the honest expression of one's innermost (and most honest) feelings. According to Bruce Lee:

> *The simple truth is that these opinions on such things as racism are traditions, which are nothing more than a "formula" laid down by these elder people's experience. As we progress and time changes, it is necessary to reform this formula. For example, some people fight with others because they believe in different religions. If, however, they only gave the matter a bit of thought, they would never fight for such a foolish cause. I, Bruce Lee, am a man who never follows the formulas of the fear-mongers. So, no matter if your color is black or white, red or blue, I can still make friends with you without any barrier.*

Bruce Lee believed that "under the heavens there is but one family." Here, proud father Bruce holds one of the two beautiful children he helped bring into the global family—his newborn daughter, Shannon (circa 1969).

But What About the Children?

Bruce Lee was born an American citizen in San Francisco, son of a celebrated Chinese father and a beautiful Eurasian mother. Linda Emery was born in Everett, Washington, the daughter of parents of Swedish–English–Irish stock. Their diverse blood lines met in their son, Brandon, and their daughter, Shannon. The result, as most who have met or seen the children would agree, is superb.

Yet shortly after the birth of Brandon on February 1, 1965 (Shannon was born on April 19, 1969), there were people who felt compelled to ask: "How will you bring up your son in a world in which prejudice is everywhere?" Lee answered the question by recounting an appropriate Chinese folk tale:

> There was a fine butcher who used the same knife year after year, yet it never lost its delicate, precise edge. After a lifetime of service, it was still as useful and effective as when it was new. When asked how he had preserved his knife's fine edge, he said. "I follow the line of the hard bone. I do not attempt to cut it, nor to smash it, nor to contend with it in any way. That

would only destroy my knife." In daily living, one must follow the course of the barrier. To try to assail it will only destroy the instrument. And no matter what some people will say, barriers are not the experience of any one person, or any one group of persons. They are the universal experience. I will teach Brandon that everyone—no matter who he is or where—must know from childhood that whatever occurs does not happen if the occurrence isn't allowed to come into the mind.

In Chinese variety stores we have a weighted dog, like your weighted clowns, which points out a moral: "Fall down nine times, but rise again ten times." To refuse to be cast down, that is the lesson. More than instructing Brandon in such precepts, I will teach him to walk on. Walk on and he will see a new view. Walk on and he will see the birds fly. Walk on and leave behind all things that would dam up the inlet or clog the outlet of experience.

I'll tell him [that he must not] enter into anything with a totality of spirit. Something must be held back. The Occidental homily is "Don't put all your eggs in one basket," but it is spoken of material things. I refer to the emotional, intellectual, spiritual. I can illustrate my beliefs by what I practice in my own life. I have a lot to learn as an actor. I am learning. I am investing much of myself in it, but not all. Gung fu is also a vital part of my life.

Finally, through all Brandon's education will run the Confucianist philosophy that the highest standards of conduct consist of treating others as you wish to be treated, plus loyalty, intelligence, and the fullest development of the individual in the five chief relationships of life: government and those who are governed, father and son, elder and younger brother, husband and wife, friend and friend. Equipped in that way, I don't think Brandon can go far wrong.

Racism in Hollywood

Apart from teaching his children how to deal with racism, Bruce Lee had to contend with the problem himself when he was offered the role of Kato in *The Green Hornet* TV series. He made it clear that he wasn't interested in playing a subservient role that would only serve to further perpetuate the Chinese stereotype personified by the character of Hop-sing in the TV series

The day before Lee recorded his famous "Lost Interview" with Canadian journalist Pierre Berton, he received the news that he'd lost the lead role in what turned out to be the **Kung Fu** *TV series. Lee held that such things as racism couldn't hold one back if the individual was true to his or her innermost self.*

Bonanza. Lee indicated that he had to lay down certain ground rules if he was to play the role of Kato:

> It sounded at first like typical houseboy stuff. I told William Dozier [the show's producer], "Look, if you sign me up with all that pigtail and hopping around jazz, forget it." In the past, the typical casting has been that kind of stereotype. Like with the American Indian. You never see a human being Indian on television.

Years later, racism cost Lee the lead role in the TV series *Kung Fu*, a series that he had helped to create. He had received the news about losing the lead the day before he sat down to record his famous *Lost Interview*. The reason he lost the role? Not that he wasn't right for the part, but because he looked "too Chinese" for an American audience to accept. As always, Lee took the news without gnashing his teeth or venting his wrath. He knew that such behavior would not alter what had happened, and that the incident pointed to a societal problem that was far bigger than the American television industry. His viewpoint was, as always, philosophical:

> *I had already made up my mind that in the United States, something about the Oriental—I mean the true Oriental—should be shown. I mean it has always been the same thing: the pigtail and the bouncing around saying "Chop-chop" with the eyes slanted and all that. And that's very, very out of date. But the question as to how an American audience would react to an Oriental lead in a TV series was discussed, and that is why my involvement in the series is probably not going to come off. Unfortunately such things [as racism] do exist in this world, you see. Like, in certain parts of the country, right? They think that, business-wise, it's a risk—and I don't blame them. I mean, in the same way, it's like in Hong Kong; if a foreigner came here to become a star, if I were the man with the money, I probably would have my own worries about whether or not the public acceptance would be there.*

But true to his philosophy, Lee offered a message of hope to all those who had been the victim of racial injustice. He believed that the individual represented the whole of mankind and that the happiness, the knowledge, and the meaning that we long for and seek from so many divergent sources outside of ourselves ultimately reside within us all. The only way, he believed, to overcome injustice was through being true and honest to your innermost self—your soul: *"It [racism] doesn't matter. Things will be all right, because if you honestly express yourself, how people perceive you doesn't matter, see? Because you will be successful. You're going to do it!"*

When asked by an interviewer in the same discussion if he thought of himself as Chinese or North American, Lee's reply was short, to the point, and philosophically dead-on: *"Neither. I think of myself as a human being."*

CHAPTER NINE
CHALLENGES

*A*re you able to take care of yourself in a real fight?" asked Hong Kong–based British journalist Ted Thomas. The man to whom the question was directed was Bruce Lee, the premiere martial artist of the twentieth century. Lee smirked slightly, put his left index finger up to his lip in thought, and then answered: *"I will answer first of all with a joke, if you don't mind. All the time, people come up and say, 'Bruce, are you really that good?' I say, 'Well, if I tell you I'm good, probably you will say that I'm boasting. But if I tell you I'm no good, you'll know I'm lying.' "*

After chuckling with Thomas over his joke, Lee then changed his jovial tone: *"Okay, going back to being truthful with you, let's put it this way: I have no fear of an opponent in front of me. I am very self-sufficient, and they do not bother me. And should I fight, should I do anything, I have made up my mind that, baby, you had better kill me before I get you."*

The point being that, as capable as Bruce Lee was of settling a confrontation with his fists or feet, his confidence in his ability to take care of himself—against anybody in the world—meant that he never felt the need to have to prove himself to anyone other than himself.

I recall an anecdote relayed to me by Lee's attorney, Adrian Marshall. The two of them had gone out for lunch with film producer Raymond Chow at an upscale Westwood restaurant. "During the course of the lunch, we were served by a jerk of a waiter who went out of his way to be rude to Bruce," recalled Marshall. "He spoke in a condescending manner to Bruce, who, to my surprise, just smiled at the man and totally ignored his rudeness. I finally asked Bruce why he put up with this jerk. Bruce replied: 'I came in here in a great mood, so why would I choose to allow someone to ruin it?'

When Bruce Lee was in a great mood, he refused to let anybody pull him out of it.

"This simple event made quite an impression on me. No purpose whatsoever would have been served by Bruce becoming disturbed by the antics of a moron—particularly one he could have destroyed in an instant. Bruce's state of security was such that this impertinent behavior couldn't offend him even slightly."

Unfortunately, many individuals don't share Lee's detached cool when it comes to such situations. Many feel that they have to put others in their place at the slightest perceived insult or threat in order to make sure that others realize that they're not to be messed with. Lee would have considered this to be a monumental waste of energy. Such a response could also be considered a sign of mental weakness, since you are, in effect, letting somebody else's impulse or desire control your own will. After all, it's you who chooses to fight or refrain, to argue, or to stew about something. Nobody else on earth possesses the innate power to make you do anything you don't choose to do.

The question underpinning all of this, however, is, Are you really secure within yourself? If you are, then you will look upon your need to defend yourself from similar impertinencies with a confidence as cool and calm as Bruce Lee's.

The ultimate goal of all human beings, according to Bruce Lee, was self-improvement and, from this, self-knowledge. This being the case, the question that one must ask oneself is, What can I do today to improve *my* understanding of myself and, as a result, to become a better human being?

Lee, in an interview given in Hong Kong in 1971, was asked to present his attitude toward people who constantly tried to "prove themselves" by challenging him. His response, I believe, bears serious consideration from all of us who are too easily upset by the remarks of others:

> *These people who make challenges must have something wrong in their hearts. For if their heart was right, they would not challenge other people to fight. Moreover, most of these people you mention who challenge me do so because they feel insecure and want to use a fight with me as a means to achieve some unknown aim. Today everything can be settled by law. Even if you want to avenge your father, you need not challenge one to a fight. When I first learned martial art, I too challenged many established instructors. But I have learned that challenging means one thing, but how you choose to react to it means something else entirely.*
>
> *What is your reaction to it? How does it get you? If you are secure within yourself, you treat it very, very lightly because you ask yourself: "Am I really afraid of that man? Do I have any doubts that that man is going to get me?" And if you do not have such doubts and if you do not have such fears, then you should certainly treat it very lightly.*

Lee then served up a metaphor that underscored his own personal way of looking at life's darker periods. It is one that all of us would do well to remember whenever life's road seems a little too steep to climb: *"It's just a case of learning to look at hardship as if today the rain is coming on strong, but tomorrow, baby, the sun is going to come out again."*

In other words, much of what we let bother us are things that, in reality, are temporary in nature, and like a rainstorm, their presence merely makes our surroundings seem bleak for a time. But in keeping with the nature of an intense rain, intense adversity cannot last indefinitely, and with its passing comes the benediction of the sun, which restores the natural balance of life. Both harmony and adversity are required for spiritual growth just as both rain and sunlight are required for biological growth. Problems and solutions are complementaries to one another, just as the sun complements the rain to complete the growth cycle. Problems and solutions. Yin/Yang. Mutually dependent and the way of all things.

CHAPTER TEN
STRESS RELEASE

*I*n keeping with his observance of the principles of Yin/Yang, Bruce Lee held that the mind and body were two halves of one totality. In other words, mental well-being has to be balanced by its complementary, physical well-being. To this end, Lee's personal philosophy evolved with an eye toward maximizing both components of the greater whole. An integral facet in the cultivation of these two constituents is the relief of both physical and mental stress, which Lee considered obstacles that stopped up the natural and universal flow of life. Unplugging these blockages through physical activity, according to Lee, resulted in a more joyous and stress-free existence.

The late pioneer of stress-research, Dr. Hans Selye, went on record as stating that mental stress can lead to a host of physical malfunctions, ranging from heart attacks to alcoholism and obesity. Conversely, Selye believed, the

Lee was a firm believer in all forms of physical fitness—including yoga. Here he assumes the lotus position on a dock during a calm afternoon on Lake Washington, Seattle.

relief of stress can go a long way toward relieving such problems. People associate stress with work and noise, but stress is also caused by intense exercise, the threat of physical danger, an injury such as a cut finger, or the sight of an old friend. Selye discovered that the body reacts the same to pleasure and success, failure and sadness. In other words, what we perceive as good and bad experiences can and do cause stress, and in fact, everyone is under some degree of stress even when asleep. Stress, then, correctly defined, is simply the wear and tear upon the body of life experiences, and its effects depend on how successfully we are able to dissipate the energy such experiences cause our bodies to accumulate.

Certainly, the release of these dammed-up emotions on a regular basis is beneficial, and clearly exercise is the best means to this end. We know, for example, that we live in a mechanical, push-button age in which everything is done for us. We ride on escalators and in elevators, cars, buses, and taxis. We sit in front of our television sets with remote control in hand for hours on end. "Life is movement," as the famed European strongman and author Eugene Sandow once pointed out, and unless we use our muscles, we will deteriorate and become old before our time. A lack of exercise actually slows down the circulation of our blood and deprives our cells of sufficient oxygen to function optimally. Many people who suffer from chronic fatigue have indicated that they actually feel *too tired* to exercise, but by releasing their tensions through activity, they invariably find that their energy levels have increased along with their stamina and that they feel more energetic afterward.

The Mind/Body Connection

It was no accident that Bruce Lee was one of the most vital human beings to ever walk the planet. He was constantly exercising in an attempt to realize the absolute limits of his physical potential. Lee's passion for training stemmed from the realization that with each progression he made physically, he was learning more about himself spiritually (in terms of adding to his understanding of both his limits and his capabilities); this resulted in a more heightened state of self-knowledge or, in Lee's terms, "spiritual awareness."

Lee told interviewer Ted Thomas in 1971: *"The most important thing to me is, How, in the process of learning how to use my body, can I come to understand myself?"*

While Lee was an ardent physical fitness aficionado, it is beyond the scope of this book to delve deeply into his complete approach to training, health, and physical fitness. For our purposes, we will do better to focus here on one single but very important aspect of Lee's physical fitness regimen—static contraction—and its role in the dissipation of stress.

Static Contraction

Bruce Lee placed a high premium on the value of static contraction exercise, not only recommending it specifically for his students but also incorporating it into his own training. It is certainly one of the easiest answers for anybody who is looking for a more convenient way to be physically fit. Anyone, from child to senior citizen, can benefit from Lee's program of static contraction exercises, and in terms of convenience, it's truly a method of exercise that has no peer—all it takes is a total of three minutes a day! Another convenience factor to consider is that these simple exercises can be performed anywhere and at any time (you can do them in your bedroom, hotel room, or living room)—and under almost any conditions.

Lee's personal program of static contraction requires no real skill to speak of. It doesn't take much practice, and, in fact, it's one of those rare activities that you actually can do well the very first time. It is also a private activity, and like running (of which Lee was also an ardent devotee), the competition, so to speak, is against only yourself. The sessions are short, and the results are quick to reveal themselves. There exists no need to change into expensive workout clothing, and there is no perspiration as in exercise with movement. Additional pluses are that there are no fancy exercise machines you need to purchase, nor any hefty membership fees to lay out to join the local health club. As for the time investment, nothing has yet to compare with this simple and yet highly effective form of exercise, as, again, only *three minutes* of exercise performed every morning will increase your overall health to a remarkable degree.

The rewards of incorporating stress-relieving exercises into his daily schedule were many for Bruce Lee—they included providing a more healthful environment in which to raise his children.

The Benefits

The benefits to be obtained from the performance of these simple movements are many; properly performed, static contraction exercise will effectively exercise the body, mind, and chi forces, or vital energy, within us. In exercising the body, it relaxes all the major muscle groups, with gentle, slow, and sustained contractions and relaxations, which can go from simple to complex depending on individual preference and intensity generated. Regular static contraction exercise will further serve to strengthen the muscles, ligaments, and tendons. It also strengthens the heart (which is itself a muscle) and will improve the circulation of the blood to the extremities.

In exercising the mind, each movement focuses the attention on the body part that is being targeted, thereby shutting out all distracting thoughts, and thus relaxing the mind while improving mental focus. With regard to cultivating our warrior, or chi, forces within, the performance of these movements will deepen our breathing to the abdominal area, as opposed to the more conventional chest area. The advantage of using the diaphragm area rather than the chest when inhaling and exhaling air is simply that the former method empties the lungs and fills them more efficiently and thoroughly. The practical medical benefits of this are obvious. But the effects of the exercise on the beginner go much further. By breathing in deeply through the nose and exhaling through the mouth, taking care all the while that the chest remains still and unexerted and that the stomach does the work, the individual can increase his flow of chi, with all of the advantages of powerful inner calm that it supplies.

These movements also exert a powerful effect on our central nervous system, as one must concentrate the mind, free it of distractions, seek tranquillity during relaxation, and apply consciousness when contracting the muscles. Such tensing and relaxing can be accomplished only under the direction of the brain, which in turn affects the central nervous system.

Additional benefit is worked upon the circulatory and respiratory systems, internally affecting the vital energy, and externally the muscles, bones, and skin. Respiration should be deep, long, natural, and gentle, concentrated on the lower abdominal area, or what the Chinese call the *dan tian* region, in an even and regular respiration that combines movement of the diaphragm and abdominal muscles. Such movement improves blood circulation, dilates the coronary arteries, and strengthens oxidation.

Although Bruce Lee himself performed many variations of static contraction exercise (from tensiometers to power rack isometric programs), certainly the program selected as the focal point of this chapter is one of the most convenient and effective for the purposes of stress release. It consists of a mere four static contraction exercises, plus two conventional exercises, for a total of six movements altogether. The beauty of this program, apart from its brevity, is the wide range of benefits that it provides. Plus, it's recommended that you perform it in the comfort of your own bed!

This form of exercise can be as mild or as severe as you desire. If you are already quite fit, make the contractions maximal, as hard as you can squeeze. If you are far from fit or somewhere in between, just perform these movements by tensing the muscles until firm and then sustaining this contraction for the prescribed period of time.

The Program

According to Bruce Lee's own directions, every day before getting out of bed, the student is to perform the following static contraction routine:

1. **Full body stretch.** Perform 5 full body stretches: Extend your legs as far as you can in one direction, and reach your arms as far as possible in the opposite direction. Maintain each stretch for 3 seconds and then relax for 2 seconds. Total time: 25 seconds.

2. **Back arches.** Perform 5 back arches: Bend your legs until the backs of your thighs are just touching the backs of your upper calves, and then slowly push your hips upward toward the ceiling while simultaneously flexing your buttocks muscles and pushing gently with your legs. Maintain each arch for 3 seconds and then relax for 2 seconds. Total time: 25 seconds.

3. **Leg tensing.** Perform 12 leg tenses: Slowly extend your legs as far as you can, and then tighten the muscles of your thighs. Maintain this fully contracted position for 3 seconds and then relax for 2 seconds. Total time: 60 seconds.

4. **Abdominal tensing.** Perform 10 abdominal tenses: Deliberately and fully contract your abdominal muscles in a manner similar to what you would do if (please forgive the imagery) you were having a bowel movement. Maintain this maximal contraction for 3 seconds and then relax for 2 seconds. Total time: 50 seconds.

Bruce Lee placed considerable emphasis on the abdominal region, considering it to be the most important area to keep fit and healthy. In a newspaper interview in the early 1960s, Lee commented: *"My strength comes from the abdomen. It's the center of gravity and the source of real power."*

At this part of the program, Lee recommended that the student "taper off" with two additional abdominal exercises performed in the standard (or nonstatic contraction) way:

5. **Sit-up touching toes.** Perform 5 sit-ups touching toes: Simply place your back flat upon your mattress with your legs fully extended in front of you and your arms extended behind your head. Now, slowly raise your torso, reaching forward with your hands until they come into contact with your toes. Hold this position briefly, and then return to the starting position. Total time: 10 seconds.

6. **Bent leg raises.** Perform 5 bent leg raises: Place your back flat upon your mattress with your arms outstretched behind your head. Slowly bend your legs and draw them up toward your chest, pausing briefly once they have been drawn as far back as possible. Return your legs to the starting position. Total time: 10 seconds.

That marks the end of the session. Total time: 3 minutes.

It should be made clear at this point in the proceedings, however, that this is not an exercise routine that is geared to make you as lean, muscular, or powerful as Bruce Lee. Lee had specific exercises (and plenty of them) that he incorporated into his personal training routine to achieve specific fitness results that he, as a practicing martial artist, required. The exercises that I've just listed were prescribed by Bruce Lee simply as a very effective method of releasing stress from the body, while simultaneously cultivating exceptional total health and fitness benefits for body, mind, and spirit.

Part Three

THE WARRIOR WITHIN

According to the Taoist perspective, the real genesis of creation was an organic process. In the beginning was *wu-ch'i* (the void, or nonbeing), and out of the void evolved two processes of energy—Yin and Yang. The interaction of Yin and Yang produced chi

*Demonstrating the core tenet of jeet kune do by reacting—instantly—to any opening the moment it presents itself, Bruce Lee (right) fires a hook kick toward the head of Korean hapkido exponent Won In Sik during a scene from Lee's third Chinese-language film, **The Way of the Dragon** (released in North America as **Return of the Dragon**).*

energy that, by pulsating at varying frequencies, became the energy that formed the universe and hence became the sine qua non of all creation—rocks, plants, solar systems, and all aspects of the human animal, from muscular activity and DNA to thoughts and spiritual awareness.

It was in the realm of the spirit that the force of chi was to manifest most readily in Bruce Lee. While he is well known for being a warrior in the combative, physical sense of the term, those who knew him best maintain that his true strength resided within. Indeed, the warrior of Lee's soul was the indomitable force driving his every action, and Lee was fully cognizant of its significance, causing him to comment on its vitality in a letter to an old friend in Hong Kong in September 1962:

> *I feel I have this great creative and spiritual force within me that is greater than faith, greater than ambition, greater than confidence, greater than determination, greater than vision. It is all these combined. . . . Whether it is the godhead or not, I feel this great force, this untapped power, this dynamic something within me. This feeling defies description, and there is no experience with which this feeling may be compared. It is something like a strong emotion mixed with faith, but a lot stronger.*

This "warrior within" that Lee had tapped into gave him complete and total confidence in achieving anything he set his mind to:

> *When you drop a pebble into a pool of water, the pebble starts a series of ripples that expand until they encompass the whole pool. This is exactly what will happen when I give my ideas a definite plan of action. Right now I can project my thoughts into the future. I can see ahead of me. I dream (remember that practical dreamers never quit). . . . I am not easily discouraged, readily visualize myself as overcoming obstacles, winning out over setbacks, achieving "impossible" objectives.*

Once Lee got in touch with his true self, he never swayed in his conviction to maintain that connection and to allow it expression whenever possible, whether through the medium of film, his relationships with friends and family, or in his practice of martial art, which he labeled "the art of expressing the human body." It is important, at this juncture, to recognize that jeet kune do, or "the way of the intercepting fist," consists of both a martial art, which has physical discipline and various combative techniques as its nucleus, and a philosophy that both underpins and interconnects the practitioner to a higher spiritual awareness.

As it is beyond the context of this book to cover the mechanics of Bruce Lee's martial art in anything approaching the depth such an exposition would require, I would like instead to examine the philosophical component of jeet kune do in this chapter, as viewed within the context of the Taoist principles conveyed in Chapters 2 through 5.

Let it be settled that Bruce Lee was a man of totality (i.e., body, mind, and spirit). Let it be further settled that, because he was also a teacher, or *sifu,* he sought to cultivate the fullest understanding of each of these components in his students. He did not want people to look upon his teachings as simply another style of martial art, because to label such a personal process of self-development a "style" was restrictive and not at all conducive to individual growth in any meaningful way.

In fact, the various styles of the martial arts can, when looked at in a certain context, be viewed as forms of *applied racism,* as most styles consider their art—and the country of its origin—superior to all others. The reasoning was, and to a large extent still is, circular; Japanese karate is the best *because it's Japanese*; Korean tae kwon do is superior *because it's Korean*; kali and silat are superior *because they are Filipino.*

To be sure, you will hear other rationalizations delivered by the proponents of each style as to why it's the best, such as "Tae kwon do emphasizes the use of the feet, because, after all, the legs are the longest weapons of the body and therefore should be emphasized in order to better one's chances of striking first without suffering being struck in return," or "Ju jitsu is the best art because 90 percent of all real fights end up on the ground." But if pressed further, the proponents will always revert back to a question of race and/or tradition—it's the best because it's Brazilian, Chinese, American, Japanese, Indonesian, or Korean. However, upon seeing the big picture, you quickly realize that these are not valid reasons so much as they are unconvincing attempts at justifying myopia, and Bruce Lee was keenly aware of this fact.

As in the formulation of his world view, Lee didn't look at styles individually but rather collectively, in their totality, seeing the common denominators that connected the best components of all styles—much like his metaphysics connected all races. The common thread of humanity connected the various races, while the common threads of physics and physiology, kinesiologically speaking, connected the patterns of combative movement advanced by these various pockets of humanity. Lee's response to the question of which style was the most effective was answered brilliantly and precisely by Lee in a Radio Hong Kong interview in 1971, in which Lee told British broadcaster Ted Thomas:

> *My answer to that is this: there is no such thing as an effective segment of a totality. By that, I mean that I personally do not believe in the word* style. *Why? Because unless there are human beings with three arms and four legs, unless we have another group of beings on earth that are structurally different from us, there can be no different style of fighting. Why is that? Because we have only two hands and two legs. The important thing is, how*

While Bruce Lee was well adept at all forms of kicking, such as the flying side kick pictured here, he also realized that even the greatest kickers needed to balance their arsenal with a sufficient repertoire of hand techniques and grappling skills in order to become complete martial artists.

can we use them to the maximum? . . . Because of styles, people are sep-
arated. They are not united together because styles became law. The origi-
nal founder of the style started out with hypothesis, but now it has become
the gospel truth, and people who go into that [style] become the product of
it. It doesn't matter how you are, who you are, how you are structured, how
you are built, or how you are made . . . it doesn't matter. You just go in
there and become that product. And that, to me, is not right.

To the rationalizations delivered by the various styles in defense of iso-
lationism, Lee would have concluded that they were simply effective *segments*
of a much greater *totality* of combat. While Lee might have concurred that
kicking does in fact make use of the body's longest weapon and that if somebody decides to take a punch at you, your leg can hit him, being the longer
weapon, well before his punch could reach you, he also would have pointed
out that there are a host of variables that such a segmented viewpoint fails
to account for. For example: What if you're grabbed by the legs before you
can get your kick off? What if you're leg becomes injured? What if you *miss*
with your kick? Obviously in any of these scenarios, the kicker would be at
a disadvantage and would be left with no means to defend himself.

Those who specialize in grappling or ground fighting take particular
delight in pointing the above out to their friends who specialize in arts that
favor kicking. The grapplers, however, are just as guilty of myopia as any of
the others. Take for example their proposition that "90 percent of all street
fights end up on the ground." This is a very interesting statement in light of
the fact that 100 percent of all street fights start *standing up*—so what's one
to do if one finds oneself in the unfortunate position of squaring off against
a fellow who fights in that "rare" 10 percent? Or what if you're grappling
away fabulously on the ground when suddenly three of your opponent's
friends show up? What then? Again it's another case of putting all of one's
eggs in one basket.

Bruce Lee's advice to these martial artists was far more philosophical: be
a balanced martial artist and look at the big picture—not any one style—for
your answers: *"As far as other styles or schools are concerned, take no thought of*
who is right or wrong or who is better than. Be not for or against. For in the land-
scape of spring, there is neither better nor worse. The flowering branches grow nat-
urally, some long, some short."

To Lee, no one approach contained all the answers. While there can be valuable methods for certain individuals in certain styles, this doesn't mean that these methods are universally applicable to all individuals, nor that they are valid in all areas of combat—the greater "totality" to which Lee referred.

"The trouble is that circumstances must dictate what you do," Lee pointed out. *"But too many people are looking at 'what is' from a position of thinking 'what should be.'"*

In noncombative terms, always try and take in the much broader picture of whatever it is you happen to be involved in, and bear in mind that no one system, leader, or sage is likely to have all the answers to your problems. Remember the backdrop of the Yin/Yang concept of never going to extremes; by remaining neutral, you are empowered with all aspects of nature's totality. Lee likened the partiality of many of his contemporaries in the martial arts to the age-old problem of *tse,* the attempt to force unnatural rules or restrictions on people. To unite with Tao, one must be in accord with *wu-tse,* through the nonstriving nature of wu-wei. To this end, he drafted a fascinating philosophical treatise, which he called *The Three Stages of Cultivation.*

The Three Stages of Cultivation

Bruce Lee believed that knowledge and proficiency in any endeavor (including martial art) consisted of three stages, which he called the three stages of cultivation:

The first stage is the primitive stage. It is a stage of original ignorance in which a person knows nothing about the art of combat. In a fight, he simply blocks and strikes instinctively without a concern for what is right and wrong. Of course, he may not be so-called scientific, but, nevertheless, being himself, his attacks or defenses are fluid.

In other words, it is a stage of innocence, of not being familiar with the subject matter before you. Your responses are natural and reflexive—honest, in other words. However, as you lack the requisite knowledge and conditioning, they are often inappropriate. With more practice and focused concentration, however, you soon enter the second stage:

The second stage—the stage of sophistication, or mechanical stage—begins when a person starts his training. He is taught the different ways of blocking, striking, kicking, standing, breathing, and thinking. Unquestionably, he has gained the scientific knowledge of combat, but unfortunately his original self and sense of freedom are lost, and his action no longer flows by itself. His mind tends to freeze at different movements for calculations and analysis, and even worse, he might be called "intellectually bound" and maintain himself outside of the actual reality.

This stage of sophistication (which Lee also referred to as "the stage of art"), is a necessary step toward one's personal evolution. Although it is confining by nature (i.e., it instructs you in *how* to act, thereby confining the individual to a particular approach), it is a necessary evil, in that along with the "conditioned response" it cultivates, it also plants the root of truth for the successful acquisition and application of higher intuitive knowledge in the fertile field of the subconscious. The individual, however, is incapable of seeing it at this stage and, instead, simply takes pride in having learned to ape what he or she has been shown is the "correct" way to do things. But subconsciously, a more significant form of learning has taken place with the development of proper neuromuscular pathways. In other words, the technique learned is not correct because your teacher has said so, but rather because it complied with a certain universal order of validity—reality, as it applies to your particular discipline. Once proficiency has been achieved in the second stage, the individual is ready to evolve to the third—and highest—stage of learning, the stage of second innocence, or "artlessness":

The third stage—the stage of artlessness, or spontaneous stage—occurs when, after years of serious and hard practice, the student realizes that after all, gung fu is nothing special. And instead of trying to impose on his mind, he adjusts himself to his opponent like water pressing on an earthen wall. It flows through the slightest crack. There is nothing to try [to] do but try to be purposeless and formless, like water. All of his classical techniques and standard styles are minimized, if not wiped out, and nothingness prevails. He is no longer confined.

This third process, as you might have ascertained, requires a return to the original stage of innocence—a return to your true self, in other words. In order to better comprehend these core principles of the jeet kune do philosophy, it may prove helpful to look at an application of them in a non-martial arts setting. Let's consider the case of Herb.

Herb hated the idea of learning how to dance, but his wife, Marge, was tired of staying home every weekend. After all, she reasoned, the children had all grown up, and there had to be more to life than simply doing the gardening and watching television. Herb was reluctant to comply, but not wanting to upset his wife—a woman he'd loved for more than forty years—he grudgingly went along with her to attend his first dance class. Gloria, the instructor at the dance academy, welcomed Herb and Marge to their first class. "When one decides they wish to learn to dance, the first thing to do is to learn the steps," explained Gloria, who then proceeded to instruct the pair in the most rudimentary of dance maneuvers.

Herb hated it. "Can't do it and look like a damned fool trying," he told his wife while soaking his blistered feet the day after his first lesson. Still, he persisted. Gradually, over a period of several weeks, Herb familiarized himself with the basic moves and found that he no longer had to concentrate so demandingly on them. In fact, he didn't have to pay attention to them at all; he just needed to listen to the rhythm and beat of the music. Soon he found his feet moving to the varied rhythms almost of their own accord. Herb grew to enjoy his Saturday nights with Marge at the dance hall. He even got creative and would throw in a few fancy steps here and there that he'd created himself. Marge would laugh and so would Herb—they were having a great time.

Herb then went back to the dance class to learn different modes of dance, and while he noted that the steps and rhythms differed from dance style to dance style, he also found that the underlying process involved in learning each of them was the same. That is, at first Herb *knew nothing* about the particular dance he wished to learn (the stage of ignorance). Then he *learned how to perform* the intricate dance steps (the stage of sophistication). After he had familiarized himself with the basic moves, he found that he no longer had to pay attention to them anymore; he was able to simply *let himself go* with the flow and rhythm of the music (the stage of artlessness).

Bruce Lee noted this three-stage process of knowledge acquisition in all those who came to him for instruction in his revolutionary martial philosophy of jeet kune do. At first, they would find the moves difficult to execute. Then they became easy. Finally the moves simply became an extension of themselves, effortless and fluid in their execution. He noted that in the final stage of jeet kune do, there was nothing to try to do. Your technique, your opponent—and even yourself—were all forgotten. Everything simply flowed together into one harmonious whole.

Looking beyond the forms through which this philosophy is revealed (i.e., in our scenarios, martial art and dance), we observe that there is a common denominator running through both that is itself an incredibly potent prescription for developing competence in any endeavor we decide to pursue.

In a letter drafted to a friend and student named George Lee (no relation), Lee asked him to create three signs that could be hung on a wall to symbolize the three stages of cultivation. The first sign consisted of one red half and one gold half of the Yin/Yang symbol with no dot in either half. This served to illustrate extreme polarity, where not even the suggestion of a component's opposite was present in either half. The two halves, to further underscore this point, were then detached from one another. The caption to this sign, Lee indicated, should read:

PARTIALITY—THE RUNNING TO EXTREME

The second sign consisted of the Yin/Yang symbol as it is commonly rendered, only in Lee's chosen colors of red and gold with a dot of gold in the red half and a dot of red in the gold half. Lee then added the arrows around the parameters to indicate the principle of Yin and Yang turning into one another endlessly. The caption on this sign read:

FLUIDITY—THE TWO HALVES OF ONE WHOLE

The third sign was simply a blank board with nothing on it except the phrase:

EMPTINESS—THE FORMLESS FORM

In other words, this is the return to nothingness—or rather, "no-thing-ness"—the return, as it were, to the stage of innocence, a stage where there exists no partiality, no segmentation or bipolar filter through which to view reality. It is a transcendence and extension of the self beyond its limited partial identity to its ultimate connection with the greater universal whole.

To further underscore this evolutionary process, Bruce Lee created a unique ranking system for his art of jeet kune do. A white or blank circle represented the first rank—the pure beginner. The next six ranks were represented by Yin/Yang symbols of varying colors. But the eighth and highest rank, like the first rank, was symbolized by a white circle. This simple yet profound symbolism reflected Lee's thorough understanding of the highest and most profound principle of Taoism: the principle of *wu-ch'i,* or the "nothingness terminus."

According to Taoists, the blank or white ring represents the nothingness terminus, which is inclusive of everything. The white circle indicating the first rank of jeet kune do indicates that the student is completely ignorant of martial art and knows no styles at all. (This is the nothingness terminus, the formlessness of the stage when the student possesses no real skill.) The diagram of the T'ai-Chi, or Yin/Yang, indicates the acquisition of skills, the understanding of the various principles of motion and tranquillity. The T'ai-Chi symbols represent all of the principles of force production/motion and relaxation/tranquillity that underlay all "styles" of combat.

Finally, if he is persistent and dedicated enough, the student of jeet kune do finds that he can transcend all styles and forms—having thoroughly comprehended the universal principles that regulate all forms of combat, and, indeed, life itself—and can move intuitively yet correctly, striking or avoiding blows at will. This stage is represented by the white or blank circle, which is now not considered to be nothingness but rather "no-thingness," indicating that the student has transcended "things"—or, in this case, "styles"— and is now possessed of deeper insight; he is "all styles" or "all things," and is therefore bound by no particular "way" of doing things or looking at life. To further emphasize this principle, Lee placed Chinese characters around the circumference of his jeet kune do emblem that read:

USING NO WAY AS WAY;

HAVING NO LIMITATION AS LIMITATION

Jeet kune do—the philosophy—was a process, a rung on the ladder of self-discovery and spiritual growth. As it was a means to getting in touch with your innermost being, it followed that there was no "way" that it could be systematized for the purpose of instruction. In other words, it was a means to highly individual ends, and one could no more pass on one's jeet kune do experience to another person than one could eat another's food for him. As Bruce Lee told *Black Belt* magazine in 1971, it all boils down to liberating yourself from whatever it is that binds you:

> *You must accept the fact that there is no help but self-help. For the same reason, I cannot tell you how to "gain" freedom—since freedom exists within you—I cannot tell you how to "gain" self-knowledge. While I can tell you what not to do, I cannot tell you what you should do, since that would be confining you to a particular approach. Formulas can only inhibit freedom, externally dictated prescriptions only squelch creativity and assure mediocrity. Bear in mind that the freedom that accrues from self-knowledge cannot be acquired through strict adherence to a formula; we do not suddenly "become" free, we simply "are" free.*

Such an approach meant that Bruce Lee did not award colored belts—as other martial arts schools do—as an indicator of progress in his method of martial philosophy. Doing so, he believed, would only be rewarding and encouraging an individual's ability to "accumulate knowledge," which was definitely a step in the wrong direction:

> *Learning is definitely not mere imitation, nor is it the ability to accumulate and regurgitate fixed knowledge. Learning is a constant process of discovery—a process without end. In JKD [jeet kune do], we begin not by accumulation but [by] discovering the cause of our ignorance—a discovery that involves a shedding process.*

The key to this shedding process lies in the pragmatic intuition born of the three stages of cultivation. If, for example, a specific way of doing things was found to work well for an individual, then he should incorporate it into his own life. If it did not work, then it should be discarded. This principle can be applied to anything, from combat to successful job hunting. If you find something that you like or, more important, that is functional for you, reduce it down, component by component, until you discover its essence, or

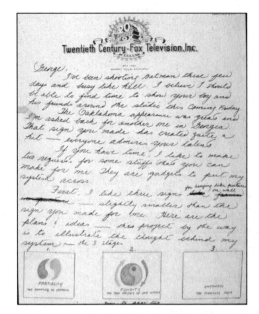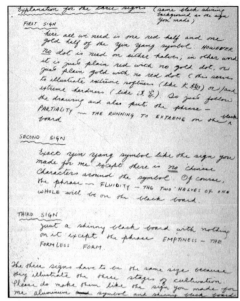

An excerpt from Bruce Lee's letter to George Lee requesting three signs representing the three stages of cultivation. These signs hung in Lee's Chinatown school during the late 1960s.

root—the axiomatic primary of what made for its effectiveness. Once this is discovered, you are in a position to improvise within these parameters of effectiveness and, ultimately, refine the component to better suit your own individual temperament and natural flow.

Bruce Lee worked overtime to quantify and formulate this process into a four-step guide to self-enlightenment that would ultimately come to define the very essence of jeet kune do:

1. Research your own experience.
2. Absorb what is useful.
3. Reject what is useless.
4. Add what is specifically your own.

This, then, was Bruce Lee's personal prescription for individual growth. If we can apply these four principles to any activity or endeavor we engage in, we will be far richer, both creatively and spiritually. The ability to be able to apply such principles to the daily situations we encounter cultivates a unique perspective that ultimately leads to the creation of significant and productive human beings, people who are contributors to art, literature, the sciences—to culture. This is not to imply that what works well for one man will necessarily work with equal results for another. Lee offered no cookie-cutter, one-size-fits-all philosophy. In other words, Lee believed that self-knowledge is an experience that each person must undertake for themselves. Truth, then, is *experiential*, it can no more be "infused" through one person to another than one can *experience* London in any meaningful way by simply viewing the snapshots of a friend who traveled there on holiday. In fact, another sign that Lee had made up addressed this very issue even more specifically:

THE TRUTH IN COMBAT IS DIFFERENT FOR EACH
INDIVIDUAL IN THIS STYLE.

Again, he warned about the dangers of assuming that the pattern of action taken by successful individuals was the sole factor responsible for their successes: *"My followers in jeet kune do, do listen to this . . . all fixed, set patterns are incapable of adaptability or pliability. The truth is outside of all fixed patterns."*

The foundation upon which the entire conceptual framework of the jeet kune do philosophy was built and shall remain is a sort of Taoist pragmatism. That is to say, you must be so in tune with yourself—the real you—that you are able to discern the answer to the questions, Will it work for me? Will it lead to my benefit? If the answer is no, then moving immediately to principle three, reject it as useless. If, however, there is something in what you are experiencing that you can acknowledge as having potential, then absorb it as being *useful* and move on to principle four by cultivating it, carefully examining its various applications until you've adapted and modified it into something that is your own creation and usable for your own personal benefit.

If you recall Bruce Lee's lessons learned at sea while sailing on the junk, he discovered the true nature of Tao, or the spontaneous natural workings of the universe as a whole. He carried this lesson into everything he did, including the formulation of his own personal form of self-expression, jeet kune do:

Jeet kune do is training and discipline toward the ultimate reality in combat. The ultimate reality is simple, direct, and free. A true jeet kune do man never opposes force or gives way completely. He is pliable as a spring and complements his opponent's strength. He uses his opponent's technique to create his own. You should respond to any circumstance without pre-arrangement; your action should be as fast as a shadow adapting to a moving object.

You must by now recognize the lesson of wu-wei, as well as the principle of "bend and survive," in Lee's words. Appropriately, the realization of these two principles requires the incorporation of a third—wu-hsin. Lee held that the best way to experience this natural process was to simply relax, thereby easing the burden of intense concentration, and focus: *"Not being tense but ready. Not thinking yet not dreaming, not being set but flexible—it is being wholly and quietly alive, aware and alert, ready for whatever may come."*

According to Lee, to realize the Way of the Intercepting Fist required this condition of wu-hsin. One simply had to have an *empty mind*. Not just thinking about nothingness which, obviously, still involves thinking *about* something (namely, the process of trying—or wei—to envision nothingness). He held that everything in the universe was related to everything else in the universe in some capacity; there was always give *and* take, and both were necessary and mutually dependent components of the whole and greater scheme of things.

Accordingly, the wu-hsin a jeet kune do student sought was well represented by Alan Watts' famous story of the centipede. As Lee explained it:

The many-footed creature was asked how it managed to walk on all of its feet without getting them tangled up. When the centipede stopped to consider how it managed this daily function, it tripped and fell. And so, life should be a natural process, in which the development of the mind is not allowed to throw the natural flow of life out of balance.

Once one has reached a level where one is in touch with the Tao, one falls into the flow of *li*, which is one's own, natural organic pattern of self evolution, and movement appears natural and effortless—because it is—thus enabling the individual to perform many complex maneuvers on an almost subconscious level of operation. At this stage of awareness, there exists no need to continue to stockpile additional knowledge like sandbags. Instead, it is now time to empty your cerebral warehouse so that you are not carrying excess baggage with you like a millstone as you climb on to still higher levels of personal evolution.

The true tao of jeet kune do* then, at least according to Bruce Lee, lies not in a process of accumulation, of the adding to your inventory of more and more factual knowledge, but rather in elimination. The idea is to seek the root or common denominator in all things—as they are revealed to you, personally—and then employ this knowledge as you see fit and of its own accord, like echo following sound, or shadow following subject. As Bruce Lee once wrote: *"In jeet kune do, it's not how much you have learned, but how much you have absorbed from what you have learned. It is not how much fixed knowledge you can accumulate, but what you can apply alively that counts. 'Being' is more valued than 'doing.' "*

Lee's point is well taken. You may well be able to read Shakespeare's plays, you may be able to quote Voltaire or Russell or some new philosopher; but if you yourself are not intelligent, if you are not creative, then what was the point of this education? According to Lao-tzu:

—48—

The pursuit of learning is to increase day after day.
The pursuit of Tao is to decrease day after day.
It is to decrease and further decrease
until one reaches the point of taking no action.
No action is undertaken,
and yet nothing is left undone.[1]

As cited in Chapter 6, Bruce Lee believed that the height of intelligence was this principle of nonstriving, or wu-wei; of not attempting to cut against the grain of the true nature of things. In attempting to comprehend the philosophy of jeet kune do, you must learn to see things in their totality, not in isolation. This does not just apply to martial arts, obviously; we, as human beings, are part of a greater totality as well. You must have a quantum perspective, in other words.

---

*The phrase *tao of jeet kune do* is actually a misnomer as *do* and *tao* are the same thing. *Do*—pronounced "doe" is simply the Cantonese rendering of the Mandarin *tao*. *Jeet kune do* is translated as "the way of the intercepting fist"; thus the *tao of jeet kune do* is rendered "the way of the way of the intercepting fist."

The Quantum Perspective

The word *quantum*, in the context of our discussion, refers to the entire measurement of nature—reality in its completeness. It includes not only the larger, more obvious, familiar world around us, but also the subatomic world, right down to the most irreducible level of transition. At such a refined level, everything appears and operates far differently from how we perceive it through our segmented perspective. There exist no solids or immutable objects. Instead, there exists a world of infinite and dynamic energy; one minute a particle is a particle, the next it is a wave, and then it's just a shape in a vast and infinite field. In this quantum world, which we touched upon briefly at the end of Chapter 3, the totality or wholeness is the greater picture—the metaphysical reality—although we cannot observe it.

Our senses, for example, report to us that we are the owners of a solid body and that it exists as such in time and space, and yet as Deepak Chopra, M.D., has indicated (and reaffirmed in virtually all of his landmark books):

> This is only the most superficial layer of reality. . . . Your body appears to be composed of solid matter that can be broken down into molecules and atoms, but quantum physics tells us that every atom is more than 99.9999 percent empty space, and the subatomic particles moving at lightning speed through this space are actually bundles of vibrating energy.[2]

In other words, while we may think of ourselves as separate from the ground we walk upon or the chair upon which we sit, and while we may believe that these entities, including ourselves, are clumps of separate matter, nothing is separate from us at the quantum level. The quantum field exists in, around, and through all of us, and we are not independent segments but part of an interconnected and far greater totality. Therefore, if we are but a microcosm of the metaphysical universe that sustains us, then the objects we view in reality are likewise.

There can be no disconnected aspects of the greater whole, in other words. Everything is part of everything. We and the universe are whole and uncomplicated. This applies particularly to matters of consciousness, which is simply a product that grows out of the world we live in. To Bruce Lee's way of thinking, knowledge is easily obtained, consisting almost entirely of the art of simplification: *"The height of cultivation is really nothing special. It is merely simplicity, the ability to express the utmost with the minimum. It is the halfway cultivation that leads to ornamentation."*

In referring this principle to the martial arts, Lee once told his student Daniel Lee:

Here it is: If you can move with your tools from any angle, then you can adapt to whatever the object is in front of you, and the clumsier, the more limited the object, the easier it is for you to pot-shot it. That's what it amounts to! Really, what it is is that it utilizes the body to come to some sort of a realization in this regard as to whatever your pursuit might be.

The entire concept of simplicity, of seeing through the veneer to the common denominator that connects the greater totality, was perfectly expressed by Lee during an earlier interview that appeared in the November 1967 issue of *Black Belt* magazine:

The extraordinary part of it lies in its simplicity. Every movement in Jeet Kune Do is being so of itself. There is nothing artificial about it. I always believe that the easy way is the right way. Jeet Kune Do is simply the direct expression of one's feelings with the minimum of movements and energy. The closer to the true way of Gung fu, the less wastage of expression there is.

Lee then went on to elaborate on this "simple" concept:

The best illustration is something I borrowed from Ch'an (Zen). Before I studied the art, a punch to me was just a punch, a kick just a kick. After I learned the art, a punch was no longer a punch, a kick no longer a kick. Now that I've understood the art, a punch is just a punch, a kick just a kick.

Let us carefully examine this statement—using martial art as metaphor— in order to fully grasp its significance. Lee mentioned that before he studied martial art, a punch to him was "just a punch" and a kick was "just a kick," for that's as it appeared to an eye that had not been trained in the martial arts. After many years of serious study of the martial arts, however, Lee could see that there did exist both subtle and not so subtle differences in the way these punches and kicks were executed within various styles. He could see, for example, the difference in the way a kick was thrown within the Muay Thai kickboxing style, the Korean art of tae kwon do, and Goju Ryu karate. He could also discern the differential between punches from Western boxing, Wing Chun gung fu, kenpo, and so on. Then, after he looked at the mechanics underlying all of these nuances, he realized that the difference lay not in the "styles" that developed these various kicks but rather in their kinesiological root or mechanical common denominator that differentiated an efficient technique from an inefficient technique.

In effect, his research and training had led him full circle, for he realized now that after all his labors and studies, a punch was just a punch and a kick was, ultimately, just a kick. This insight caused him to draw what, in the martial arts world of the late 1960s, was a very revolutionary conclusion indeed: *"Man, the living creature, the creating individual is always more important than any established style or system."*

When asked in 1972 to explain this statement, Lee provided the following answer:

> *I mean this: I mean that man is always in a learning process. Whereas "style" is a concluding, established, solidified something, you know? I mean you cannot do that, because you learn every day as you grow on, grow older. Each person must not be limited to one approach. We must approach it with our own self, you know? Art is the expression of ourselves, whereas if you go to, say, a Japanese style, then you are expressing the Japanese style— you are not expressing yourself.*

Self-expression, as we shall see in the following chapter, was the top of the mountain, as far as Bruce Lee was concerned.

CHAPTER TWELVE

YOU ARE IT

*More and more . . . it's becoming more and more simple to me as a human
being. And more and more I search [within] myself, and more and more the
questions are more and more listed. And more and more I see clearly.*

BRUCE LEE

∞

he route to enlightenment and true peace of mind consists of self-
knowledge or, as Bruce Lee referred to this phenomenon, "spiritual realization." In a letter Lee once wrote to a friend in Hong
Kong, he commented on the productivity and enjoyment one could experience by learning to tap into this inner warrior:

> *Before he passed away, someone asked the late Dr. Charles P. Steinmetz,
> the electrical genius, in his opinion, "What branch of science would make
> the most progress in the next twenty-five years?" He paused and thought
> for several minutes, then like a flash replied, "Spiritual realization." When
> man comes to a conscious vital realization of those great spiritual forces within
> himself and begins to use those forces in science, in business, and in life,
> his progress in the future will be unparalleled.*

It was important to Lee that we learn to marshal this inner warrior, or
"great spiritual forces within," in order to better understand the universe

without—and our role in it. In other words, from an understanding of self proceeds an understanding of others and of the way of our world generally. Lee realized that the universe, being self-regulated, flowed according to wu-tse, or nonmandated rules, and was therefore indifferent to our individual desires and hopes. This is a fact of reality that is palpably obvious: people whom we dearly love eventually pass away; promotions we sincerely want and that would represent a dramatic change in lifestyle for us don't always come our way; and for every prayer answered, millions go seemingly unheard. The universe, then, for all of its grandeur and glory, remains beyond our volitional control.

Still, as Francis Bacon once pointed out, "Nature to be commanded, must be obeyed," and this, to Lee, indicated that if we could unite with Tao, if we could learn the way that the universe operates and our role within it, we could also learn what powers, if any, we possessed to engineer certain aspects of our lives within the parameters of our li, in order to maximize our chances for long-term health, success, and survival—and, of course, to achieve that most illusive of ambitions, peace of mind. Lee said it succinctly: *"All in all, the goal of my planning and doing is to find the true meaning in life—peace of mind. . . . In order to achieve this peace of mind, the teaching of detachment of Taoism and Zen proved to be valuable."*

To this end, Lee looked to the Tao and to its conceptual underpinnings of wu-tse, li, Yin/Yang, the law of noninterference with nature, and the law of harmony. From these, Lee learned that man was a part of nature and not something to be contrasted with it, and that the purpose or meaning of one's life had to come from within, from a process of introspection and self-understanding. In other words, through a process of getting to know all there is about the *real* you, not just physically, but intellectually, emotionally, and spiritually as well.

Lee found the martial arts to be one activity that provided a means of obtaining self-knowledge in all of these categories: *"I learn martial art because I find it is like a mirror in which to reflect myself. I personally believe that all types of knowledge—I don't care what it is—ultimately means self-knowledge."*

With this understanding, Lee looked upon his martial arts instruction as a means through which one could get in touch with the warrior within, or the true self:

The way that I teach it, all types of knowledge ultimately mean self-knowledge. So therefore my students are coming in and asking me to teach them not so much how to do somebody in; rather, they want to learn to express themselves through some movement, be it anger, be it determination, or whatever. So, in other words, what I'm saying therefore, is that they're paying me to show them, in combative form, the art of expressing the human body.

According to Lee, the highest rung on the ladder of individual achievement was this commitment to honest self-expression. Its attainment, he believed, required one to become an "artist of life," the result born of a rigorous commitment to spiritual and intellectual honesty:

Basically, I have always been a martial artist by choice, and an actor by profession. But, above all, I am hoping to actualize myself to be an artist of life along the way. . . . Therefore, to be a martial artist also means to be an artist of life. Since life is an ever-evolving process, one should flow in this process and discover how to actualize and expand oneself.

The more one reads Lee's words, the more apparent becomes the supreme value he placed on utilizing art as a means to acquiring liberation and as a vehicle through which to obtain self-knowledge. Further, art—the concept—need not be looked at in purely combative (i.e., martial art) terms. If you recall the point drawn in Chapter 1 regarding the true meaning of gung fu, you will remember that it is manifested in any thing or activity through which one reveals self-mastery. Certainly this was Lee's belief, as he held that an artist could be anyone from a modern dancer to a film director. In commenting on the nature of art and its relation to self-knowledge, Lee penned the following thoughts:

Art calls for complete mastery of techniques, developed reflection within the soul.

Art is an expression of life and transcends both time and space. Behind every motion is the music of the soul made visible. Art reveals itself in psychic understanding of the inner essence of things, and gives form to the relation of man with NOTHING, with the nature of the absolute.

Creation in art is the psychic unfolding of the personality, which is rooted in the Nothing. Its effect is a deepening of the personal dimension of the soul. *

In this respect, Lee held that artistic skill, per se, did not mean artistic perfection, since art, by definition, is ever evolving—a process, in other words, steps in one's own psychic development. This being the case, the perfection of such a process cannot be found in structured methods or techniques but must instead radiate from the human soul. According to Lee: *"Artistic activity does not consist in art itself, as such. It penetrates into a deeper world in which all art forms of things inwardly experienced flow together, and in which the harmony of soul and cosmos in the nothing has its outcome in reality."* *

The famed Greek philosopher Plato (427–347 B.C.) in one of his dialogues compared the human soul to a chariot that was pulled by two horses in opposing directions. The chariot's driver, representing our control center, he likened to Reason, and the two horses were Spirit (which Plato considered our noble emotion) and Appetite. Bruce Lee, on the other hand, viewed the soul—or inner self—to be a synthesis of only two forces: natural instinct (i.e., our spontaneous, purer self) and control (or our logical, structured self). In his famous *Lost Interview*, Lee provided the following analogy:

On the one hand, there is natural instinct and on the other is control. You are to combine the two in harmony. For if you cultivate only one dimension, say natural instinct, you will be very unscientific. If you have the other to the extreme, you become all of a sudden a mechanical man, no longer a human being. So I strive to teach the successful combination of both. It is not pure naturalness or pure unnaturalness. The ideal is unnatural naturalness or natural unnaturalness.

It is sometimes difficult for the Western mind, with its thousands of years of conditioning in the ways of theoretical knowledge, to comprehend such a relaxed, naturalistic philosophy. Our culture does not now—and hasn't perhaps since the days of the Greeks—combine philosophy and art with ath-

---

The quiet, contented awareness with which Bruce Lee viewed life was born of his deep understanding of himself—that he was part of a vast, eternal process.

letic pursuits such as martial arts. But quite clearly Bruce Lee's attitude was that these were simply facets of the same totality:

> *To me, ultimately, martial art means honestly expressing yourself. Now it is very difficult to do. I mean it would be easy for me as a martial artist to put on a show and be cocky and be flooded with a cocky feeling at how impressive and cool my techniques would appear to you. And I could continue on in this phony way, blinded to the fact that I was doing this to impress you instead of actually expressing myself. But to express oneself honestly—not lying to oneself—and to express myself honestly, that, my friend, is very hard to do.*

So how does one learn to achieve this level of honest self-expression? According to Bruce Lee, you could learn to express yourself honestly only through a rigorous commitment to getting to know the real you and then expressing the beliefs and feelings of the real you as honestly as possible—

not expressing a transitory emotional state but your honest, innermost feelings from the depths of your very soul. This, as Lee indicated, was not an easy process. It was one that required daily training of the mind as well as of the body. Indeed, it is only through the understanding of the limits and the capabilities of the body and mind that one can truly come to any meaningful sense of spiritual realization. As Bruce Lee said:

> *You have to train. You have to keep your reflexes so that when you want it—it's there. When you want to move—you are moving. And when you move, you are determined to move! Not accepting even one inch less than 100 percent of your honest feelings. Not anything less than that. So that is the type of thing you have to train yourself into. To become one with your feelings so that, when you think—it is.*

To Lee, this was the summit of human achievement—not success, not financial rewards, not the opinion or esteem of others, but the honest expression of a human soul to a fellow human being:

> *In life, what more can you ask for than to be real? To fulfill one's potential instead of wasting energy on [attempting to] actualize one's dissipating image, which is not real and an expenditure of one's vital energy. We have great work ahead of us, and it needs devotion and much, much energy. To grow, to discover, we need involvement, which is something I experience every day—sometimes good, sometimes frustrating. No matter what, you must let your inner light guide you out of the darkness.*

In his own life, for example, Lee believed that it was all right for him to have lost the lead role in the TV series *Kung Fu*, because he knew that he had sought to develop and acquire it through honestly expressing himself. Through this process of honest self-expression, he had in effect fulfilled his duty as a human being to the fullest, and that, ultimately, was the only truly important thing.

As self-knowledge was the key required to unlock the door to li, or our *true* nature, Lee only shook his head when he saw others misjudge his message and simply try to copy the things that he did. Such behavior missed the point entirely, for it wasn't a question of being "like Bruce Lee" that was important to his success, but in *his being Bruce Lee*, in expressing fully the honest feelings, emotions, and nature of his innermost being.

In other words, Lee discovered the way to abide in the flow of his natural self-evolution without striving to force it into something that went against the grain of its own nature. Trying to become what you are not by adopting the ways or mannerisms of another person is a facade—wei, or artifice—and you should be nonstriving (wu-wei), just growing and developing in your own process. Everyone must do this for themselves. Lee attempted to explain this highly individual way of personal growth during a conversation he shared with Hong Kong broadcaster Ted Thomas:

> *When I did* The Green Hornet *television series back in 1965, I looked around and I saw a lot of human beings. And as I looked at myself, I was the only robot there. I was not being myself. I was trying to accumulate external security, external technique—the way to move my arm and so on—but I was never asking: "What would Bruce Lee have done if"—the word if— "such a thing had happened to me?" When I look around, I always learn something, and that is, to always be yourself and to express yourself. To have faith in yourself. Do not go out and look for a successful personality and duplicate him. That seems to me to be the prevalent thing happening here in Hong Kong. They always copy a person's mannerisms, but they never see beyond that. They never start at the very source, the very root of their own being, and ask the question: "How can I be me?"*

Knowledge of yourself is crucial. It is more important for a human being to know himself than it is to know anything else, because it is only once you know yourself that it is possible to truly know anything else. Lee observed that too many of us look upon successful people as being the end result of a construct of correct actions. Unfortunately, while this is to a large degree true, the concept of "correct actions" will vary with each individual. The lock to the door of ego, or self-consciousness, which separates us from our natural, spontaneous and true selves, cannot be opened by any other key than self-knowledge. There is no master key, in other words, no one-size-fits-all approach to satori.

Should you attempt to employ somebody else's way of attaining enlightenment, you end up forcing the issue (wei) and become frustrated, like trying to cram a size 9 foot into a size 3 shoe. It also leads to what the Hindus refer to as *maya* (a false image), which causes you to confuse the pretense with the genuine article. In this case, it means confusing yourself—the real you—with a false image. Then you end up spending the rest of your life mired in the illusion of dualism, losing sight of the fundamental unity of all things, with the result that you're forever trying to find the right key to open the door to what will ultimately prove to be not your true self, but an empty soul.

Bruce Lee explained the problem in the following lines from an essay he wrote in the early part of 1973, entitled "In My Own Process":

> *Most people only live for their image. That is why where some have a self, a starting point, most people have a void. Because they are so busy projecting themselves as "this" or "that," they end up wasting and dissipating all their energy in projection and conjuring up of facade, rather than centering their energy on expanding and broadening their potential or expressing and relaying this unified energy for efficient communication. When another human being sees a self-actualizing person walk past, he cannot help but say: "Hey now, there is someone* real!"

Lee felt that anything which substituted the ways or beliefs of others in the place of teaching you how to cultivate your own was a step in the wrong direction. For this reason, Lee was opposed to the doctrines—or rather the dogmas—of organized religion.

When asked by journalist Alex Ben Block in the summer of 1972 what his religious affiliation was, Lee answered: *"None whatsoever."*

Block then pressed him further, asking him if he then believed in God: *"To be perfectly frank, I really do not."*

Lee's responses to these questions are perfectly understandable given the depth and nature of his philosophy. Lee believed that we are beings of self-made soul that were part of a vast, eternal process. Therefore, any person or organization that held creed or, in the martial arts nomenclature, style as the ideal was moving in the wrong direction, away from spiritual growth and knowledge of self. Lee told Canadian journalist Pierre Berton:

Styles tend to . . . separate people—because they each have their own doc-
trine, and then the doctrine becomes their gospel truth that you cannot change.
But if you do not have styles, if you just say "Here I am, as a human
being—how can I express myself totally and completely?" if you can do this,
then you won't create a style, because style is a crystallization. This way
is a process of continuing growth.

To therefore spend time looking for something supernatural—by definition, beyond the natural world—for answers to this world's problems involves
the age-old difficulty we encounter whenever we try to understand nature
by stepping back from it, rather than simply living our lives within its dictates. While certainly the idea of a supernatural father figure in the sky offers
enormous comfort and appeal to many of us in the West, Lee was more interested in affairs that were closer to home, such as getting in touch with his
inner energy cycles and discerning their relationship in the quantum scheme
of things.

Lee was once asked by his younger brother Robert if he believed in God,
to which he replied, *"I believe in sleeping."*

Years later, I had the chance to ask Lee's son, Brandon, what his philosophy of life was. He thought for a moment, and then a mischievous smile
played about his lips as he said, "Eat—or die!"

While these remarks of both father and son might read somewhat glib,
both reveal the real-world nature of Bruce Lee's philosophy, which is that
our concerns while we live in this world should deal with matters pertaining to our survival in this world, our relationship to others in this world,
and the environment that has produced us. In these self-governed, though
interconnected, relationships, there is nothing that stands apart from nature
in order to direct it as we in the West envision the deity.

It hearkens back to Bruce Lee's analogy involving Kwan-yin in Chapter
3. The body is a self-governing organism, and the universe is simply an extension of the body. Ergo, the universe is a self-governing organism, an organic
process that is known in Chinese as *tzu-jan*, or "of itself so."

It seems, then, that Wittgenstein was right after all, at least in terms of
universals. The world is truly all that is the case (although, perhaps, he
would have been better advised to have simply left it at that). In other words,
we as individual human beings are simply cogs in the cosmic wheel we call

the universe. We are part of a natural process. That is to say, we—all of us—are part of the world and not something separate, something that stands in abstraction, like a detached island, either off to the side or on high within a kingdom in the clouds. We have grown out of the world like the millions of other life forms that surround us, and therefore, we cannot possibly be above or independent from the natural laws that regulate it in a manner that is "of itself so." In this respect, the solutions to "this-worldly" concerns are simple, not unlike Lee's earlier recounting of the Zen maxim: "In summer we sweat, in winter we shiver."

We need adequate rest to function to the fullest capacity of which we are capable, and if we don't get enough to eat, we die.

If it all seems rather simple that's only because it is. The idea is to reduce the superfluous to see the truth, a process of discarding until we understand. Some have problems with such a perspective, as the absolute simplicity of it all can prove to be uncomfortable and occasionally hard to fathom. As Bruce Lee himself concluded: *"It is indeed difficult to convey simplicity."*

The entire hypothesis of religion and supreme beings with divine plans, by definition, deals not with this-worldly concerns and life as it *is* and presently flows through us. Instead, it deals with otherworldly hypotheses of spiritual kingdoms and discerning the rules and requirements for entrance into them. It is predicated on the world view that the universe is monarchical in structure, presided over by the Judeo-Christian deity as the heavenly father. Such a concept is, as we learned in Chapter 3, the antipathy of Lee's view of the world as democratic, self-regulating, and organic in nature.

Lee did not believe, for example, that we—that is, our true selves—are somehow *put into* this world so much as we *grew out of it*, in exactly the same way as every other organism that shares space with us on the planet. (Note: see Alan Watts' extract from his essay "Eco-Zen," in the appendix of this book, for a full elaboration of this position.) Again, there is no experiencer apart from the experience, and the mental detachment required to contemplate such *otherworldly* concerns is yet another means of abstraction that causes us to stand back from life in its suchness for the purpose of analyzing.

Bruce Lee believed that one should simply live life—not analyze it. While analyzing creates vexing problems, living life makes us more like the willow, with the result that we are free of spiritual burden. To this end, Lee held that the real you was the Self (with a capital S), what Alan Watts called "the self of the universe." At this most irreducible level of one's existence, one is not at all separate from everything else that is happening at the moment.

Lee's philosophy provides a means of liberation from excessive self-consciousness, which is why his "way" does not consist of believing in any credo, of performing any rituals, or of obeying some authority figure. What Lee posed was simply a means of correcting one's spiritual eyesight through a correction of the astigmatism of ego, or self-consciousness. According to Lee: *"What man has to get over is the consciousness—the consciousness of himself."*

While this process requires a certain amount of time to cultivate, Bruce Lee held that it is not simply a question of age or, as some are fond of calling it, maturity.

> *There is no such [thing] as maturity. There is instead an ever-evolving process of maturing. Because when there is a maturity, there is a conclusion and a cessation. That's the end. That's when the coffin is closed. You might be deteriorating physically in the long process of aging, but your personal process of daily discovery is ongoing. You continue to learn more and more about yourself every day.*

Success and Philosophy of Life

Bruce Lee believed that self-knowledge and success were interrelated. Self-knowledge was simply an accurate means by which to comprehend the world around us and thereby its ways and means. Lee viewed life as a process, and despite his incredible success and global popularity, his philosophy allowed him to keep a level head when, at times, the world around him seemed to be going mad. In an essay written in early 1973, entitled "Another Actor Speaks His Mind," Lee expressed this insight: *"Dedication, absolute dedication, is what keeps one ahead. A sort of indomitable obsessive dedication and realization that there's no end or limit because life is an ever-growing process, an ever-renewing process."*

The key to success, then, lies in the wisdom and the inner contentment derived from learning to understand—and to live *with*—nature's ways, abandoning all artifice and false or useless knowledge, and replacing these with a trustful acceptance of nature's wisdom and feeling, in a humble and unpretentious imitation of nature's silent dictates. Bruce Lee read Lao-tzu and well understood this passage from the sage:

—37—

The Tao never does anything,
yet through it all things are done.

If powerful men and women could center themselves in it,
the whole world would be transformed
by itself, in its natural rhythms.
People would be content
with their simple, everyday lives,
in harmony, and free of desire.

When there is no desire,
all things are at peace.[1]

A group of "seekers": Bruce Lee with some of his jeet kune do students, including Kareem Abdul-Jabbar (directly behind Bruce), Daniel Lee (kneeling, far left, front row), and Daniel Inosanto (standing directly to the left of Bruce Lee)—all training to "search internally for the cause of their ignorance."

Lee believed, however, that while we are still alive, it is our duty—if we are to fulfill ourselves as human beings—to seek to understand ourselves, discover ourselves, and to express ourselves honestly and to the fullest extent of our individual potential. In this process of evolution, true progress is possible. True, it will not always result in spectacular and world-renowned success, but it will lead to two things that are far more valuable—truth and peace of mind. As he put it: *"I have said before. 'Truth is nowhere to be found on a map.' Your truth is different from . . . mine. At first, you may think that this is truth, but later you discover another truth and then the former truth is denied—but you are closer to truth."*

The function and duty of what Bruce Lee would term a "quality" human being was the sincere and honest development or actualization of our individual and unique potential. It's not an easy process by any means, as often the road we travel in our quest for self-actualization is littered with detours that will take us up the opposite path of self-image actualization—a thing to be avoided entirely. In a portion from an essay written near the end of his life, Bruce Lee wrote down the following thoughts to himself as a means of explaining what he had learned during his own personal process of self discovery:

I have come to discover through earnest personal experience and dedicated learning that ultimately the greatest help is self-help; that there is no other help but self-help—doing one's best, dedicating one's self wholeheartedly to a given task, which happens to have no end but is an ongoing process. I have done a lot during these years of my process. As well in my process, I have changed from self-image actualization to self-actualization, from blindly following propaganda, organized truths, etc., to search[ing] internally for the cause of my ignorance.

It is through Bruce Lee's example of successfully finding the cause of his personal ignorance that we are inspired today to continue searching for the cause of our own.

CHAPTER THIRTEEN
THE ART OF FIGHTING—
WITHOUT FIGHTING

*T*here is a tremendous scene in Bruce Lee's last completed film, *Enter the Dragon*, which perfectly expresses the highest purpose of his art and philosophy of jeet kune do. The scene has Lee on a large junk that is sailing from Hong Kong to an island destination, the locale of a brutal martial arts tournament presided over by Han, the renegade Shaolin Temple monk who has turned to a life of crime.

On the junk, a New Zealand martial artist begins to flex his martial muscle, attempting to intimidate his fellow passengers, some of whom will be his opponents in the forthcoming tournament. He chooses to do this by picking on and brutalizing the smaller Chinese stewards and cabin boys. After kicking a basket of fruit out of one's hands and then side-kicking him across the deck of the boat, he focuses on Lee, who is standing, unbelligerently, looking out across the waters. He attempts to goad Lee into a duel on the boat. Lee ignores him. Incensed, yet curious, the martial artist asks him: "What's your style?"

Lee smiles at the question. "My style? You can call it the art of fighting without fighting."

This intrigues the martial artist. "The art of fighting—without fighting? Show me some of it!"

Sensing that his adversary is not to be dissuaded and that some action must be taken, Lee agrees—with the proviso that they not fight aboard the junk. "Don't you think we need more room?" Lee asks.

"Where else?" comes the martial artist's reply.

Lee smiles again as his eyes return to scanning the ocean. They come to rest upon a sandy cove. "That island—on the beach," says Lee, who then gestures to the lifeboat that is attached to the junk. "We can take this boat."

Nodding in agreement, the martial artist says: "Okay."

As Lee works to unfasten the rope securing the boat to the junk, the martial artist steps into it. At that moment, Lee lets the line play out in his hands setting the martial artist adrift at sea. Lee had no intention of ever joining the man at all. His swiftness of thought had given him victory without his once ever having to throw a punch or kick. He had, in fact, won the battle through the use of "the art of fighting without fighting."

The Cry of the Soul

Let us examine this principle in a little more detail through a similar lesson taught in the Japanese art of fencing known as kendo. *Ken* is Japanese for "sword," while *do* (pronounced "doe") is the Japanese word for "way" or "tao." Taken collectively then, the term is rendered "the way of the sword." This may come as a surprise to some of us in the West, as we wonder how the pacifistic philosophy of Tao could ever be connected with anything so ferocious as the art of sword fighting. However, it must be remembered that warfare in all of its forms is simply applied Yang, a necessary and therefore desirable component of the universe—if, of course, its presence is counterbalanced by its complementary, Yin.

Interestingly enough, shortly after Zen Buddhism was introduced into Japan it became the favorite philosophy of the fearsome samurai, the feudal warriors who were for many centuries involved in perpetual civil war between the various feudal lords of Japan. And as the samurai lived in constant danger and insecurity, they took up Zen as a way of inner peace in the midst of outer turmoil. Thus, the way of the sword became deeply imbued with Zen concepts, and this was especially apparent in the warriors' use of a *kiai*, a "fighting yell" that is employed in an attempt to throw an opponent off psychic center.

You are probably familiar with the various fighting yells emitted by Bruce Lee during his films. Lee's films—at least the ones in which his authentic war cries are used—leave the viewer with a profound impression. He incorporates a high-pitched shriek, not unlike the wail of a wild cat combined with the shrill shriek of an enraged bird. I remember, years ago, my martial arts instructor telling me that Lee's war cries were high-pitched in order to evoke the mental image of a hysterical woman and a wild animal, two sounds that evidently, would serve to terrify an opponent and cause him to tense up, which, as we shall soon learn, is a component of Taoism applied to combat.

The tale exists of an aged Chinese Taoist master named Lin-chi (known in Japan as Rinzai), who, when people would ask him "What is the meaning of Taoism?" would respond with a loud scream. The people who came to him for enlightenment were, needless to say, rather nonplussed, as this is typically not the way one would answer such a question (although one suspects that Bertrand Russell, the famed Cambridge mathematician and Nobel Prize winner, might have enjoyed such a prank). However, this response was in fact a trap set by Lin-chi to see if the questioner could be fazed and thereby thrown off center.

In the same way, Bruce Lee would use a similar terrifying shout during combat to startle his opponents into losing their psychic balance and thinking for a moment. Lee knew that if he could cause his opponent to think, that would, perforce, cause hesitation or pause—and this hesitation would create just the opportunity Lee needed to attack successfully. The moral is that one must learn to flow in the natural Tao—without once hesitating or pausing. So it is in all martial arts, most notably, perhaps, in jeet kune do, where there is to be no interval between attack and defense. Good martial artists in combat seem to almost dance together and appear to be going through the motions as one body—until that one critical moment where one man pauses to think, loses his guard, and is thereby done for.

This attitude is called in the Chinese *mo chih ch'u*, which means "going straight ahead" without pause or hesitation. There is a Zen poem attributed to the famous Japanese swordsman, Miyamoto Musashi, which says:

> Under the sword lifted high
> Is hell making you tremble;
> But go straight ahead
> And there is the land of bliss.

In other words, become fluid motion with no stoppage or hesitation, become a nonfixated response to the moment.

This characteristic is particularly evident in Bruce Lee's films when he finds himself surrounded by several opponents. He doesn't hesitate and wonder, "How shall I respond to this attack?" because if he did, he would, in effect, be concentrating too much on defending himself against one opponent on only one side. His mind, in other words, would be stuck on that one opponent, with the result that he could be caught unaware by an attack from the other side. Instead, Lee displays the necessity of cultivating what he called "an unstuck mind," the ability to be alert and instantly responsive to the entire situation around him.

> *A gung fu man's mind is concentrated by not dwelling on any particular points of the opponent. This is especially true when dealing with many opponents. A gung fu man's mind is present everywhere because it is nowhere attached to any particular object. And it can remain present because, even when related to this or that object, it does not cling to it. The flow of thought is like water filling a pond, which is always ready to flow off again. It can work its inexhaustible power because it is free, and be open to everything because it is empty.*

In other words, if your mind gets fastened at any particular point, whether in combat or in an argument, you can, in effect, be caught by that point and defeated. And so an "unstuck," or nonanalytical, mind is the fundamental requirement, not just for the successful martial artist but also for the individual who is looking to go through life without being bogged down in a quagmire of perpetual problem solving.

This concept has its referent in the realm of Japanese swordsmanship known as kendo, which we touched upon earlier, since in the hands of a man who is adept in both Tao and kendo, the sword can, in an interesting irony, become a symbol of nonviolent resistance. In fact, the highest school in kendo is actually known as the "No-Sword School," and there is a relevant anecdote regarding this school that will instantly bring to mind the "art of fighting—without fighting" scene described above, from the film *Enter the Dragon*.

According to the tradition, there was a great samurai traveling on a ferryboat, and just as they were putting off from shore, a drunken, rowdy samurai stepped onto the ferry and started bragging about his prowess with a sword.

He turned to the first samurai and said: "Well now! What is your school of swordsmanship?"

The first samurai answered: "My school is known as the No-Sword School of swordsmanship."

This intrigued the rowdy samurai, who then said disdainfully: "Show me the method of this No-Sword School!" and he immediately drew his sword to challenge the first samurai.

Rather than responding in kind, the first samurai said, "I would be happy to show you my No-Sword School method, but if we fight on this boat, we might hurt innocent bystanders. Why don't we go and fight on that island over there?"

The rowdy samurai agreed that this would be a better locale for combat, so he instructed the ferryman to take the boat over to the island. When they arrived, the ruffian jumped off onto the island all ready to begin the fight, and at that moment, the other samurai grabbed the oar from the boatman and pushed the boat back out into the deeper waters, leaving the drunken samurai effectively stranded—and thereby defeated—on the island.

"Here," called out the first samurai, "is my No-Sword School method!"

As you can see, the highest art of combat, both to Bruce Lee and to the samurai, was to arrive at a level of such mental acuity that it would be possible for one to achieve total victory without ever having to use one's weapons. Certainly this was Lee's belief with regard to his own art of jeet kune do. In fact, to this end, Lee along with scriptwriter Stirling Silliphant, collaborated to pen these lines that were spoken during the premiere episode of the television series *Longstreet*, which aired in North America in 1971:

Lee, I want you to believe it's more than just learning how to defend myself. There were a couple of times there when you were teaching me that I felt that my body and my head really were together. It's funny that out of a martial art, out of combat, I'd feel something peaceful. Something without hostility. Almost as though if I knew jeet kune do, it would be enough simply to know it. And by knowing it, never have to use it.

CHAPTER FOURTEEN
LESSONS FROM A MASTER'S SON

*J*met Brandon Lee one time and one time only, in a small business office inside the Prime Ticket Building in Century City, California. Surprisingly, this one encounter would prove to have a profound and far-reaching impact on me personally and professionally. In many respects, the seeds of writing this book were sown at this meeting, as Brandon—with his talk of spirituality, of self-knowledge being man's metaphysical starting point, and of his interpretation of his father's philosophy of jeet kune do—put an entirely new color in my philosophical paint box, one that has remained with me ever since.

Gauging from some of the correspondence I've received over the years, my conversation with Brandon that day has had a similar impact upon others who have read portions of the edited transcripts, which have appeared in several martial arts journals. I still have the audiotape of our conversation, which I play from time to time to brush up on some of the insights that Brandon shared with me during the course of our conversation. In reviewing this material again now, it strikes me that while Bruce and Brandon shared

Brandon Lee—
an "artist of life"

many similarities, as you would expect with father and son, the most striking, I believe, was the depth of their philosophical perspective.

I was particularly impressed that hot and humid afternoon by Brandon's
absolute genuineness of soul, the almost effortless way in which he—without a trace of artifice or self-consciousness—communicated with me on such
an open, deep, and honest plane. I'll be forever beholden to him for this experience and for the lessons I learned from a master's son that day.

But I get ahead of myself. Indulge me for a moment as I recollect how
our meeting came about—or rather, how it almost didn't. I recall driving—
fast—and in something akin to a blind panic—up and down what seem to
be the thousand or so side streets that, collectively, make up that always
crowded periphery of Los Angeles known as Century City.

When I finally found the building that was to be my destination for the
remainder of the morning, it was already 11:15 A.M. Not bad time—for me.
Unfortunately, I was supposed to have been there at 11:00 A.M.—sharp. The
story of my life: I was late again.

Worse yet, I was late for an interview that I had taken great pains to set up with Brandon Lee, a person with whom I'd wanted to converse ever since I was thirteen years of age. It was at this point in my life that I had first learned of Bruce Lee and of the fact that he had died tragically young, but that his life-force had been preserved in two children, an eight-year-old boy and a four-year-old girl. I knew at that moment that one day the boy and I would meet. Why did I feel so confident about this at that time, or at that age? I have now only the vaguest of speculations, but nevertheless, it was a position I held right up until the day our lives did indeed intersect in that little office off of Santa Monica Boulevard some nineteen years later. I should mention at this point that I also have come to know Bruce Lee's "little girl," Shannon, quite well (she has grown up and blossomed into a unique and beautiful human being—and first-rate actress—in her own right), but up until that day in August 1992, the one person I had most wanted to meet for the longest period of time was Brandon Lee.

In any event, when I entered the building and cleared reception, I was told to wait in a small adjoining room by Brandon's publicist, Robin Baum, while she went to fetch the man himself. As I busied myself in preparation for the interview that was to come by checking battery levels in my tape recorder, the question sheet, and so on, the door suddenly swung open and in stepped Brandon Lee. I placed my materials down upon the surface of a large conference table that took up most of the space in the room and turned to face the "friend" whom I had never met. Brandon walked with a definite spring in his step, and his demeanor was completely relaxed and natural, a sort of wu-wei in motion. I recall keenly wanting to remember the moment of meeting, of wanting to remember such things as the establishing of eye contact and the feel of the texture of his hand as we clasped hands in greeting. I also remember being struck by the fact that Brandon had piercing green eyes, since I had fully expected them to be brown (although why I thought this, I cannot fathom).

After we shook hands, I remember that there followed a moment of silence—by no means uncomfortable—in which neither one of us said a word but remained with our eyes fixed upon one another. I felt a strange sense of familiarity with the man now standing before me, no doubt owing to the fact that I'd kept up on how his career had been progressing and had seen him grow from a child to a man through the eyes of the press. There was the brave little nine-year-old boy, holding his mother's hand in an attempt to console her at his father's funeral in Seattle; there was the proud young man who attended the premiere of what proved to be his dad's last film, *The Game of Death*; and more recently, there was the budding young superstar, ready to carve out his own niche in Hollywood. All of these images were now standing before me, incarnate, in the form of a young man ready to take on the world—on his own terms.

All of us who had been fans of his father had hoped feverishly for Brandon's arrival. Perhaps we may be forgiven our selfishness for wanting so desperately to see him succeed, to see his father's torch passed on to the only hand that was truly capable of carrying it. Naive as it may read now, part of the reason for my being there that day was, I thought, to do my part in helping Brandon receive the kind of publicity that was necessary for him to fulfill his cinematic destiny. It strikes me now as being somewhat silly that I attached such significance to an encounter that was, in all probability, simply one of dozens of interviews that Brandon happened to grant during the course of his lifetime. Nevertheless, my retrospective cynicism cannot erase the fact that this one meeting had a profound impact on my life.

Suddenly Baum reappeared and indicated that the two of us should sit down across from one another at a large oak conference table. She inquired if we would like anything to drink—such as coffee—before she left us alone to talk. We both replied in the affirmative. Brandon looked at me and said with a smile, "My only bad sin is that I drink *a lot* of coffee." As Baum left for the caffeine-laden beverages, Brandon kicked back in his chair, taking full advantage of the comfort afforded him by his casual dress that day of white cotton T-shirt and black denim jeans.

He smiled easily, sincerely, and as you might expect from one supremely confident in the mastery of their craft (or their gung fu, to keep within the theme of this book), he had an aura of confidence about him. His hair was worn rather long, and I was struck at once that, physically, Brandon's build was slight. I estimated his weight to be perhaps 155 pounds—but then, as he told me, there were reasons for his current appearance:

Right now I'm getting ready for The Crow, *so I'm just trying to get my body fat way down. It's down to about 6 percent right now, but I want to*

go, like, painfully thin, and I'm trying to do that without significantly losing a great degree of muscle mass, but it's hard because that's such a fine
line to walk.

It wasn't long into the conversation before Brandon's spin on his father's
first principle of jeet kune do ("research your own experience") became
evident:

*I respect my father very much, but I'm a very different person than he was.
I've grown up in a different country and obviously had many different influences than he had as a result. Acting, however, is something I feel I've pur-
sued to a large degree on my own. You know my dad passed away when I
was nine years old, so we never really had a chance to get into any real
deep conversations about acting or a mutual appreciation of films or anything like that. And I've had the opportunity to pursue acting in a lot of
different ways that my dad didn't have the opportunity to do, because he
got into it when he was much older than I was when I got into it.*

Brandon, obviously, was not looking for a successful personality to copy,
which, as we learned in Chapter 12, his father had identified as the wrong
approach to self-actualization. Instead, Brandon had applied the second principle of jeet kune do ("Absorb what is useful"), as it pertained to the martial arts—a practice he began at the feet of his father and that he found
particularly useful in developing in his *own* process:

*I guess the martial arts, which are an integral part of my life, come entirely
from my father. I'm completely beholden to my dad for that. I mean, he
started me in the martial arts when I could walk. He trained me my entire
life until he passed away, and then even when I continued my training, it
was with one of his students. So while I've had some different influences
throughout the course of my martial arts training, essentially the martial arts
to me is so connected to my dad that it's almost like they're not different at
all. I guess that has been his strongest influence.*

Even though Brandon learned much from his father, he also realized that
his father's message transcended his art, and Bruce Lee's call to "keep on flow-

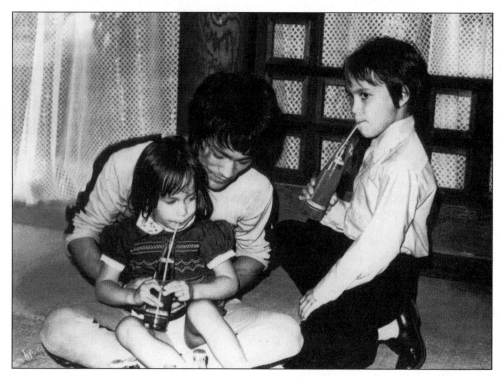

Brandon (right) and Shannon visit their father on the set of **Game of Death.** *The Lee family was always together.*

ing" was heeded by his son, who told me: *"My martial arts goal is just to keep training and keep evolving. To learn new things all the time."*

Brandon also indicated that he had been offered many roles in martial arts films that would have resulted in his following in his father's footsteps, but Brandon right away saw the limits to traveling along such a path. He knew that simply being a copy or inviting comparisons with his father would only arrest his own spiritual and artistic development, and it would prevent him from developing in *his own process.*

In other words, Brandon had decided to reject these roles under the third principle ("Reject what is useless") in order to continue evolving to the fourth principle, the summum bonum ("Add what is specifically your own"). He realized that complying with such an "easy money" request, his choice would have been based upon seeking approval from others and letting them decide how he, as an individual, should evolve. Brandon emphasized the

theme espoused by his dad—"always be yourself and have faith in yourself"—
by seeking his contentment from a source within rather than without:

> *All I can tell you is that you cannot make choices in your own career, either*
> *career choices or choices when you're actually working as an actor, based on*
> *trying to downplay or live up to a comparison with somebody else. You just*
> *can't do that. You have to do your own work based on your own gut, your*
> *own instincts, and your own life.*

Our conversation evolved in its course to the topic of psychology. It was
here that Brandon shared with me some of his more interesting insights into
the human condition:

> *It's an interesting experience that, should you ever talk to somebody who*
> *has a real big chip on their shoulder, it's like their point of view is entirely*
> *viewed through that chip on their shoulder. That's what filters everything*
> *they see. And to somebody on the outside looking at a person like that, it's*
> *so painfully obvious what they're hung up on, but to the person that actu-*
> *ally has the chip on their shoulder, it's their whole world and they can't see*
> *anything without it.*

He explained that he'd just finished the movie *Rapid Fire* and that one
of the things that had attracted him to the project was the opportunity to
play a character with just such a chip on his shoulder:

> *I think the best thing about this kid is that he gets the chance at the end*
> *of the film to kind of lift that chip off his shoulder. And you know, we've*
> *all kind of had that experience where we've kind of lifted a great weight off*
> *our shoulders and said: "Wow, it's so simple now. I can see a different per-*
> *spective." At the beginning of the film, though, he's somebody who really*
> *has that, and I liked that, because when you're playing a young character*
> *in general, which, of course, I'm going to be doing for a couple more years,*
> *oftentimes it's so hard because they don't have any history to them. I mean,*
> *how many stories does a guy who's twenty-two years old have to tell? He*
> *just doesn't have a lot of history to him. That's one reason that it's such a*

great chance to be an actor, because when you get into your thirties and into your forties, it's like "Hey, I've got more stories to give and more experiences to draw on." But this character I play did have some background. I liked the whole Tiananmen Square background [the role called for Brandon's character to witness the death of his father at the Tiananmen Square massacres], and I liked the way he got to have a genuine problem at the beginning of the film that resolved itself, in a sense, by the end—if the film works for you.

I note now, with a certain degree of pathos, that the character Brandon played in *Rapid Fire* was, in many respects, not unlike himself—at least, apropos the removal of a chip from one's shoulder. For the longest time, he was never known simply as Brandon Lee, as you or I are known by our own names. For most of his life, Brandon's name was immediately joined by the qualifier "Bruce Lee's son," and this presented no small problem to a young man struggling to find his own identity in the world.

Please do not interpret this in any way to mean that Brandon wasn't proud to be his father's son—because he most definitely was, and rightly so. In fact, he was quite vocal in acknowledging his father's positive influence on his own development and his father's contributions to the realm of martial arts, filmmaking, and philosophy. Nevertheless, Brandon recognized the absolute necessity of his own personal evolution and development outside of his father's enormous and unquestioned legacy. Brandon strove throughout much of his adult life to achieve independence of mind, body, and spirit, and through their achievement, he became liberated. Although it may sound paradoxical, it was actually through the direct understanding and application of his father's philosophy that Brandon became liberated from his father's shadow.

This process, as you are probably well aware at this point, involved his getting to know and express himself through becoming what his father called "an artist of life," and ironically, Brandon selected the same media that his father chose in order to accomplish this: the martial arts and film. Brandon focused heavily on the latter, where he knew his true passion resided. In time, he became one with his true nature, which he expressed honestly and fully in his films.

By so doing, he found peace in accepting himself for who he was, including the fact that he was his father's son. In fact, near the end of his life, he openly stated his pride in his lineage. The chip or burden, in other words, had—through a long process of self-actualization—been effectively removed from his shoulder. The issue of resolving problems through a process of self-actualization is a recurring theme in this book, and it was also a philosophical reservoir that, despite their own unique personalities, both father and son drew heavily from during the course of their respective lifetimes.

In speaking with Brandon that day, his discourse really began to sparkle when we broached the topic of the martial arts. He spoke openly about his personal training program and how he looked upon it as a means of achieving a sense of mental and physical self-knowledge:

> *I'm really interested in that point you reach when you actually fail from exhaustion at something, whether it's weight training or cardiovascular exercise. I'm interested in seeing just how much of that is a physical point and how much of it is a mental point. When you reach that point where you say, "Oh, that's it! I can't do another one," if you actually challenge yourself with something like "All right, there's a man standing with a gun to your mother's head, and he says, 'If you do one more' of whatever it is you're doing—say, jump rope for one more minute—'I won't pull the trigger, otherwise I will' "—see if you can do it! You've got to try and challenge yourself this way. I find that you have to make it into a game at some level in order to continue doing whatever foolish thing it is you're doing that's causing you so much discomfort!*

From such training experiences, Brandon learned much about himself in terms of his mental and physical limitations and the power of his mind in extending the limits of both. Brandon found in the martial arts, not just a system of self-defense but a true and profound sense of gung fu. It taught him lessons about his physicality, his emotional fortitude, and even a profound sense of spirituality: *"The martial arts is a pursuit that, in my mind, is very capable of providing some deep and lasting spiritual experiences to a person— if that person is open to them."*

I asked him how he had derived such a spiritual sense of enlightenment from the practice of such a physical activity. And at that moment, he waxed his most eloquent:

Well, I would say this: When you move down the road towards mastery of the martial arts—and you know, you are constantly moving down that road—you end up coming up against these barriers inside yourself that will attempt to stop you from continuing to pursue the mastery of the martial arts. And these barriers are such things as when you come up against your own limitations, when you come up against the limitations of your will, your ability, your natural ability, your courage, how you deal with success—and failure as well, for that matter. And as you overcome each one of these barriers, you end up learning something about yourself. And sometimes, the things you learn about yourself can, to the individual, seem to convey a certain spiritual sense along with them.

I asked him if, by spirituality, he meant one's soul in a self-knowledge sense of the term. His response proved very insightful indeed:

Yes, not only a self-knowledge but, through knowledge of self, a knowledge of others as well. It's funny how you can only see things in hindsight really, you know? You can look at someone else going through much the same thing you're going through and, only then, really see it clearly—after you've gone through it. And I think there is a certain amount of spirituality in that, as long as you continue to do that.

It's funny, every time you come up against a true barrier to your progress, you are a child again. And it's a very interesting experience to be reduced, once again, to the level of knowing nothing about what you're doing. I think there's a lot of room for learning and growth when that happens— if you face it head on and don't choose to say, "Ah, screw that! I'm going to do something else!"

We reduce ourselves at a certain point in our lives to kind of solely pursuing things that we already know how to do. You know, because you don't want to have that experience of not knowing what you're doing and being an amateur again. And I think that's rather unfortunate. It's so much more interesting and usually illuminating to put yourself in a situation where you don't know what's going to happen, than to do something again that you already know essentially what the outcome will be within three or four points either way.

There is much wisdom in Brandon's words, and upon hearing his reference to becoming like a child in order to expand one's life experiences and, hence, one's spirituality, I was immediately reminded of the words of Lao-tzu, who wrote:

—55—

He who possesses virtue in abundance
may be compared to an infant.[1]

Like his father, Brandon's insights into the human condition belied his years. To me, he appeared a wise old philosopher within a young man's body, and his discourse on these topics fascinated me. It was during this conversation, in fact, that Brandon delivered what has become his classic statement regarding the conceptual underpinnings of his father's very nonclassical martial art of jeet kune do:

You know, it's interesting. When people ask me the question in interviews, generally what my "style" is, I usually say that "my father created the art jeet kune do while he was alive and I have been trained in that." Because it's simple to say that. However, I actually truly feel that it's a little bit too simple to say that because jeet kune do was my father's very personal expression of the martial arts, and he himself actually said in one of his writings before he passed away, if jeet kune do ever becomes an issue in the martial arts world, that is, an issue to where people are saying jeet kune do is this or jeet kune do is that, or "We will form a jeet kune do school," he would rather have seen the name just pass away. Because it was never intended to become another sacred cow. I mean, he intended to kill a lot of sacred cows. So I always feel a little bit silly saying "I practice jeet kune do," although I certainly have been trained in it. It would be more accurate to say that I practice my own interpretation of jeet kune do. Just as, frankly, everyone who practices jeet kune do does—because that's what it was intended to be.

Danny Inosanto, my sifu [and the man who ran Bruce Lee's third martial arts school in Los Angeles during the late 1960s] always talks about teaching "jeet kune do concepts." In other words, teaching someone the concepts, a certain way of thinking behind the martial arts, as opposed to teaching them techniques. To me, that kind of illustrates the difference between giving someone a fish and teaching them how to fish. You could teach someone a certain block, and then they have that block; or you can teach someone the concept that lies behind such a block, and then you have given them an entire area of thinking that they can grow and evolve in themselves. They can say: "Oh, I see—if that's the concept, then you could probably also perform it this way or that way and still remain true to the concept." And that's a lot of what lies behind jeet kune do. And that is then dedicated to creating a dedicated, free-form martial artist.

Bruce Lee couldn't have said it better himself.

CHAPTER FIFTEEN
SIGNPOSTS

S ometime in early 1973, Bruce Lee drafted a letter to a young man who had contacted him with the intent of receiving instruction in Lee's martial philosophy of jeet kune do. At the time, Lee was far too busy working (i.e., producing, writing, directing, choreographing, and starring in films) to have any free time left over in which to teach. Graciously declining the request, Lee stated: "Time-wise I wouldn't have time to teach, but I'm willing—when time permits—to honestly express myself or "to open myself" to you—to act as a sort of a sign pole for a traveler."

The traveler in this case was a man named John, but Lee's advice is pertinent to anyone of us who want to travel down life's road in search of truth. Quite in keeping with his personal philosophy, Lee realized that the most enlightened form of teaching was to serve not as a "giver of truth" but rather as "a pointer toward truth," to point a student in the direction of one's own truth in the hope that the student would ultimately find his or her own. Lee put a finer point on this by adding: *"My experience will help but I insist and maintain that art—true art that is—cannot be handed out. Furthermore, art is never decoration or embellishment. Instead it is a constant process of maturing (in the sense of NOT having arrived!)."*

Lee believed that the road to truth, and from that truth to satori, had many different paths—out of necessity. People, as Lee noted earlier, are different, with different wants, desires, and aspirations, and while we all share a common biological root, the individual expression of our personalities and true selves is tremendously diverse. In his letter, Lee continued: *"You see, John, when we have the opportunity of working out, you'll see that your way of think-*

ing is definitely not the same as mine. Art, after all, is a means of acquiring 'Personal' liberty. Your way is not my way. Nor mine yours."

While a personal letter from Bruce Lee would serve as quite a signpost in guiding one along life's road, letter writing wasn't the only form of signpost that Lee chose to erect to help his students become all that they were fully capable of. He was an avid writer and note jotter, furiously scribbling down his thoughts as they percolated through his mind. The style of writing that Lee often chose to express these concepts was the time-honored Chinese style of poetic aphorism:

To change with change is the changeless state.

∞

Life is a constant process of relating.

∞

Not being tense but ready. Not thinking but not dreaming. Not being set but flexible. Liberation from the uneasy sense of confinement. It is being wholly and quietly alive, aware and alert, ready for whatever may come.

∞

Man, because he is a creative individual, is far more important than any style or system.

∞

Liberating truth is a reality only in so far as it is experienced and lived by the individual himself; it is a truth that transcends styles or disciplines.

∞

Knowing is not enough; we must apply. Willing is not enough; we must do.

∞

A good teacher protects his pupils from his own influence.

❦

True refinement seeks simplicity.

❦

It is the will that makes men—success takes perseverance.

❦

Empty heads have long tongues.

❦

If every man would help his neighbor, no man would be without help.

❦

Yesterdays dreams are often tomorrow's realities.

❦

If you want to do your duty properly, you should do just a little more than that.

❦

Pessimism blunts the tools you need to succeed.

❦

Optimism is a faith that leads to success.

❦

A goal is not always meant to be reached, it often serves simply as something to aim at.

❦

One great cause of failure is lack of concentration.

❦

Showing off is the fool's idea of glory.

❦

If you don't want to slip up tomorrow, speak the truth today.

❦

Self-education makes great men.

❦

If you think a thing impossible, you'll make it impossible.

❦

If you love life, don't waste time, for time is what life is made up of.

Even in the more mundane aspects of day-to-day life and communication, Bruce Lee was capable of stirring insight. We shall finish this chapter with Lee's own concluding words from his letter to John, in the hopes that this final signpost might prove helpful to you in your own process of spiritual realization:

Whether or not we can get together, remember well that art "lives" where absolute freedom is. With all the training thrown to nowhere, with a mind (if there is such a verbal substance) perfectly unaware of its own working, with the "self" vanishing nowhere, the art of JKD attains its perfection.

CHAPTER SIXTEEN

MARTIAL ART AS ALLEGORY—

THE FILMS OF BRUCE LEE

ruce Lee was, in the words of his senior student Daniel Lee, "a master teacher." Lee was always striving to learn something new about himself and, by extension, the world around him. He felt compelled to share the knowledge that he acquired with his friends and students. Many stories abound in the martial arts community about individuals visiting Lee at his home in Bel Air and being held spellbound into the wee hours of the morning as the master would hold forth in lengthy discourse about the ways of combat, Zen, and human relationships.

Not surprisingly, when Lee began to involve himself in filmmaking, he opted to use the medium as an instructional vehicle to educate mass audiences on various philosophical principles that perhaps, until that point, they had not considered. Lee himself said as much himself during an interview with the newspaper the *Hong Kong Standard*, during the early part of 1973:

> *It is time somebody did something about the films here [in Hong Kong]. There's simply not enough soulful characters who are committed, dedicated and are at the same time professionals. I believe I have a role here in Southeast Asia. The audience needs to be educated and the one to educate them has to be somebody who is responsible. We are dealing with the masses and we have to create something that will get through to them. We have to educate them step by step. We can't do it overnight. That's what I am doing right now. Whether I succeed or not remains to be seen. But I don't just feel committed, I am committed.*

To this end, Lee attempted to teach his Western audiences about Oriental culture, believing that fear and conflict, being born of ignorance, could be eradicated through education. The martial arts, for example, were an ostensibly Asian practice during the period in which Lee lived, but if Western audiences found them interesting, Westerners might look differently at the Asian cultures that produced these arts. Likewise, Lee's Eastern audiences might learn through the film's lessons that at least some of the ways of the West had something of value to offer as well.

The result of Lee's commitment to education was that a moral of sorts could be drawn from each film he made. As he described it: *"I hope to make multilevel films here* [in Hong Kong]—*the kind of movies where you can just watch the surface story if you want, or you can look deeper into it if you feel like it."*

This pattern became more evident with each successive film, and as he became more successful and popular, the producers and directors allowed him more latitude in which to create and express himself in his films. Many different lessons can be learned within each of Lee's films (which is one reason why they bear up so well under repeated viewings). I shall attempt to present some of the more significant philosophical lessons that can be found within his four completed films, and I'll also speculate on the lessons that *might have been*, had Lee lived to complete the film *The Game of Death*, which he had intended to be the cinematic showcase for his art and philosophy of jeet kune do.

Fists of Fury (1971)

According to Lee's friend and disciple, Dan Inosanto, Lee used *Fists of Fury* (released in Hong Kong as *The Big Boss*) to teach the combative lesson of the proper approach to mass fighting:

If you study the combative footage, you will notice that he begins by viciously attacking the first man. The object is to take the leader or best fighter out as viciously as possible to intimidate the group psychologically. Tasting his own blood with a nonplussed look of total disdain is another ploy to intimidate. If you are lucky, the group will disband demoralized. If not, you must next try to zone off to the side and create situations where you are fighting one man at a time.

The lesson actually runs deeper than this, however. It hearkens back to the Taoist concept of wu-hsin, or "no-mindedness." This does not mean a blank mind, which excludes all emotion, nor is it a case of simply possessing calmness and quietness of mind. While these qualities are important, it is the nonattaching—nonpausing to analyze an experience, entity or situation—that is the root meaning of the term. In true wu-hsin, there is nothing to try to do, for whatever comes up moment by moment is accepted—and instantly reacted to. For example, when Lee is surrounded by multiple attackers intent on doing him bodily harm, there is a calm, detached sense of awareness that comes over him. This a peripheral, nonspecific awareness that is an extension of Tao. It cannot be taught, per se, but is rather perceived. Its full impact is realized through observation of the way one reacts to the true nature of Tao. In Lee's words:

> Concentration in gung fu does not have the usual sense of restricting the attention to a single sense object, but is simply a quiet awareness of whatever happens to be here and now. Such concentration can be illustrated by an audience at a football game: instead of a concentrated attention on the player that has the ball, they have an awareness of the whole football field. In a similar way, a gung fu man's mind is concentrated by not dwelling on any particular part of the opponent. This is especially true when dealing with many opponents.

The end result is that Lee responds—instantly—like echo to sound, to any movement or attack his opponents initiate without any deliberation. In other words, because he was able to keep a detached mind during the encounter, he is able to prevail.

Another lesson taught through this film is the "art of dying," the detachment from the fear of death—or more accurately, from the fear of losing one's grasp on life. At the climax of the film, after discovering that his relatives have been brutally murdered, Lee, in a daze, wanders off to sit on the bank of a nearby river, contemplating his life and what has become of it. Suddenly he leaps to his feet and throws his personal belongings—symbol-

izing the last of his "this-worldly" attachments—into the river, thereby
effectively detaching himself from worldly concerns.

He has died to all fear of personal loss, including even the fear of losing
his life, since he has now accepted that he is effectively a dead man—and
the dead have no possessions to lose. Lee is then able to proceed, to exact
retribution from those who wronged his family, unimpeded by any concerns
or inhibitions of self. He has learned the art of dying. To quote a line of
Lee's from the TV series *Longstreet*: *"To accept defeat—to learn to die—is to be
liberated from it."*

When Lee's character accepts this, he is liberated and reborn in the
knowledge that he is no longer a powerless, isolated vessel adrift on a universal ocean, but is in fact one with the entire process. As Sir Edwin Arnold
once wrote: "Forgoing Self, the universe grows I."

The Chinese Connection (1971)

In this film, Lee taught several lessons about combat as well as making
statements about racism and moral values. The racism issue comes into play
during Lee's attempt to enter the infamous Shanghai Park, where a sign actually hung at the turn of the century proclaiming NO DOGS AND CHINESE
ALLOWED. Lee, whose core belief was that "under the sky, under the heavens there is but one family," attempts to enter the park. When he is pre-
vented from doing so and is further insulted, he takes action, indicating that
human beings should have no tolerance for intolerance. In other words,
attempting to relegate other races to subhuman status will ultimately cost you
dearly in the long run.

The film also reveals how the individual who is free to express himself
can triumph over belief systems, represented in the film by the styles of Japanese karate and Russian wrestling. The belief inherent in most styles—that
their art and its practitioners are invincible because of its national origin or
ideology—is shown to be baseless. Lee makes the point in this film that success in combat all depends on the individual—and more important, on the
will of the individual in question. As he himself once told a Taiwanese
reporter:

Lee's death leap from Golden Harvest Films' **The Chinese Connection:** *a very honorable end "according to the Chinese fashion."*

You must have complete determination. The worst opponent you can come across is one whose aim has become an obsession. For instance, if a man has decided that he is going to bite off your nose no matter what happens to him in the process, the chances are he will succeed in doing it. He may be severely beaten up, too, but that will not stop him from carrying out his objective. That is the real fighter.

In this film, and to a certain extent in all of his films, Lee teaches the Confucian ideal of repaying kindness with kindness but repaying evil with justice. The taking of a person's life is a morally wrong act, and so Lee taught the lesson through this film that one must take responsibility for one's actions—and be fully willing to pay the price for murder—no matter how justified one's crime may appear. This was actually a theme that Lee incorporated into all of his films. In fact, in a scene that Lee wrote that never appeared in his last film, *Enter the Dragon*, he had his character speak the following line: *"A martial artist has to take responsibility for himself and to face the consequences of his own doing."*

In *The Chinese Connection*, Bruce Lee dispenses justice to the Japanese martial artists who have repeatedly humiliated and murdered his fellow countrymen. However, along with his dispensing of justice comes the recognition that the process required the taking of additional lives—a morally wrong act. Lee's character, Chen-Chen, recognizes this and gallantly accepts the punishment (he bravely faces a firing squad at the end of the film). Lee commented on this component of the picture to the same Taiwanese reporter:

> *I don't believe in playing up violence. I think it is unhealthy to play up violence. . . . I don't think one should use violence and aggression as themes of movies. The glorification of violence is bad. That is why I insisted that Chen-Chen, the role I played in* Fist of Fury *[released in North America as* The Chinese Connection*], should die in the film. He had killed many people, and he had to pay for it.*

However, Lee also taught in this film that one should never go against the grain of li by opting to surrender the expression of one's true nature or development to anyone—even if the price for this natural development of spirit is death. Bruce Lee discussed the morality of this during a telephone conversation he had with friend and senior student Daniel Lee in 1971:

> BRUCE LEE: *At the end [of the film], I died under the gunfire. But it's a very worthwhile death because it means, you know, [justification] for the Ching Wu School, the Chinese, and all that. I walk out and I say, "Screw you, man. Here I come!" Boom! I leap out and leap up in the air and they stop the frame and then ba-ba-ba-ba-ba-bang!—like [the ending of the movie]* Butch Cassidy and the Sundance Kid, *except they stop the frame so that I'm in the middle of the air, you know.*

> DANIEL LEE: *It's a very honorable end.*

> BRUCE LEE: *Right—according to the Chinese fashion, of course.*

In other words, you must not be afraid of the consequences of staying to the natural course required to fulfill your ultimate potential.

Return of the Dragon (1972)

Perhaps the primary message from this film is that close-mindedness should be avoided at all costs. In one of the scenes from the movie, Bruce Lee is witnessing several individuals practicing Japanese karate in the privacy of a back alleyway. He asks the man who has ushered him to his particular vantage point if he himself practices with these martial artists. The man shakes his head. "Naah," he says disdainfully. "It's foreign!" The man, a nationalistic Chinese, has no interest in anything that's non-Chinese in nature.

Chuck Norris's downfall in Concord's **Return of the Dragon,** *caused by "looking at 'what is' from a position of thinking 'what should be.'"*

Lee takes him to task for having such a close-minded attitude: "If it helps you to look after yourself when you're in a fix, then you should learn to use it. It doesn't matter at all where it comes from. You should realize that!"

As it was Lee who wrote the script to this film, it proved to be an encapsulation of his personal philosophy of jeet kune do: because we are constantly learning, any style or system that purports to have the *final word* or *all* the answers is mistaken. In this case, there is something to be learned in every art and no one art has all of the answers for each and every individual.

Lee also emphasized the importance of imposing your rhythm on an opponent and to not let others dictate the terms—that is, if you wish to be triumphant. During the classic fight scene that Bruce Lee choreographed between himself and Tang Soo Do stylist, Chuck Norris, Lee finds himself losing until he imposes his own cadence on the fight, causing Norris to accept his terms. And because Norris's style is too rigid—and because it is the only style he has been trained in—he does not know how to step out of it or adapt to what is unfolding before him. Because of this inability to adapt, he perishes. As Lee once told a reporter from the *Washington Star* newspaper: *"The trouble is that circumstances must dictate what you do. But too many people are looking at 'what is' from a position of thinking 'what should be.'"*

Lee's position in this film is that the style of martial art that will always emerge victorious is the style of "no-style." In other words, there should be no method, as method simply traps or confines an individual. Instead, one needs options and the freedom to use them. In his words: *"There should only be tools to use as effectively as possible. The highest art is no art. The best form is no-form."*

At the end of Lee's battle with Norris, in which Lee's character, Tang Lung, is given no other choice but to kill Norris's character, Colt, Lee reveals both through expression and gesture that it was a life he did not want to take. There is a profound sense of sorrow for the loss of a human life that has chosen to take the honorable path. Colt—although hired for money in the beginning—could have thrown up his hands and quit as soon as the battle tipped to Lee's advantage. Instead, he opts to fight on, accepting the possibility of death.

There is honor in death, in other words, if one opts to die honorably. Colt's final actions were noble because they were born of moral and honest intent. Shortly after Tang Lung takes Colt's life, he picks up the top of Colt's karate outfit, or *gi*, and black belt (which were discarded prior to their engagement) and places them over Colt's body in a symbolic gesture that his opponent's soul was worthy of respect.

By this act, Lee was imparting the message that it was okay to respect your fellow man—even if that man happens to be an adversary in a life-or-death situation—if that other man is sincere in his beliefs. If people tell you only what you want to hear or if they are willing to prostitute themselves for money by fighting for a cause that they don't truly believe in, then they are unworthy of respect. But if somebody is wrong and honestly believes in his heart that he is right, like Norris's character in the film—then his actions reflect the purity and honesty of his soul, and these are two qualities that are worthy of human respect.

This is, perhaps above all of the other lessons taught in this film, the lesson that is the most significant—the lesson of honest self-expression. As Lee himself commented when asked by American journalist Alex Ben Block to reveal the plot of this film: *"It is really a simple plot of a country boy going to a place where he cannot speak the language but somehow he comes out on top because he honestly and simply expressed himself."*

When Block asked him the question, "In your films, do you express yourself?" Lee answered: "Yes—I mean honestly and as much as I can."

That Lee was successful in this regard—and particularly in this film—is beyond any shadow of doubt.

Enter the Dragon (1973)

One of the key lessons to be learned from this film became the theme of Chapter 13, "The Art of Fighting—Without Fighting," so I shall not focus on it again here. An additional lesson taught by Lee in *Enter the Dragon*, however, was one of his personal favorites—the need for honest self-expression.

At the beginning of the film, Lee is shown instructing a young martial arts student.

"Kick me," Lee says, as he assumes the on-guard position of jeet kune do. The youth delivers a side kick that is more pose than substance, hoping to impress his instructor with his form and flexibility. In this respect, he has entirely misjudged his instructor's intent.

"What was that," Lee asks, "an exhibition?"

Lee tries to impart the concept to the boy of *becoming* the technique as opposed to standing outside of the technique to admire it. True satisfaction, in other words, comes from within when you're able to give physical expression to your innermost feelings and emotions.

"We need emotional content," Lee says. "Now try again."

This time the boy is steamed. His attempt to impress his instructor obviously didn't work, and his attitude is now "If you didn't like that, wait until I drive this one right *through* you!" He fires another side kick at Lee, but because it is fired in fury, it is well telegraphed and Lee easily sidesteps it.

"I said emotional content—not anger!" Lee admonishes the young student. "Now try again—with me."

In other words, the boy's kicks should simply be involuntary, reflexive responses to Lee's movements—like echo following sound. Lee's words get through to the youth, and the boy fires two more side kicks, neither of which are telegraphed or postured in any way. They are simple, direct—and to the

"It is like a finger pointing a way to the moon. Don't concentrate on the finger or you will miss all that heavenly glory!" Bruce Lee to his young student in Warner Brothers' megahit **Enter the Dragon.**

point. Although Lee is still able to parry them, he acknowledges the boy's improvement.

"That's it!" Lee enthuses, which causes the boy to beam in accomplishment.

"How did it feel to you?" Lee asks.

This question has the same effect on the boy as asking the centipede how it walked with so many legs. Trying to buy time, he responds, "Let me think. . . ." Lee cuts him off abruptly by giving him a not so gentle slap across the top of his head in an effort to bring the boy back to the living moment—the *now.*

"Don't think—feel! It is like a finger pointing a way to the moon," Lee explains, until he notices that the boy is looking at his finger instead of to where the finger is pointing. Lee again brings him back to the now with a slap on the forehead.

"Don't concentrate on the finger, or you will miss all that heavenly glory."

The moral here is not to mistake pretty form for genuine substance, nor to let an emotional extreme be the deciding factor in your response to a situation. Instead, make your movement a "real" and an "honest" expression of your pure self by having it occur naturally, almost of its own accord, the instant that your opponent reveals an opening.

In other words, you could say that your opponent has "caused" your response, as it has occurred almost involuntarily of itself. This again is another lesson in wu-hsin—not fixating on any one object or allowing any thought process to impede your ability to react spontaneously to whatever you experience. Lee had intended to elaborate further on this lesson in a scene that was to follow in the film between him and an old Shaolin monk. The scene was—for typical Hollywood reasons—cut from the final print of the film for fear that Western audiences would not be able to comprehend it. Fortunately, inside Lee's personal copy of his script, he penned the dialogue that he created for the ill-fated scene:

OLD MONK: *Your skill is now not a matter of technology but of spiritual insight and training. I would like to ask you several questions. What was your immediate feeling toward your opponent during sparring?*

LEE: *There is no "opponent."*

OLD MONK (in a tone of anticipation for more): *And why is that?*

LEE: *Because the word* I *just does not exist.*

OLD MONK (happy at student's comprehension): *Yes!?*

LEE: *So when no notion of conflict is stirred in one's thought pattern, when one has forgotten the word* mind, *then the state of mindlessness is most fluid. When my opponent expands, I contract. And when he contracts, I expand. Then when there is an opportunity, "I" do not hit [as Lee raises his fist]—"it" hits all by itself.*

Lee also revealed in this film the necessity of being competent in all ranges of combat, with a solid repertoire of kicks, punches, throws, locks, and sweeps. In the final fight scene, Lee emphasizes that no matter how proficient you are with empty hands, you must learn to go against a weapon, because not everyone is going to fight fairly. Lee takes several cuts to show that sometimes you have to sacrifice to get someplace.

This, of course, was revealed in Lee's written teachings:

Forget about winning and losing; forget about pride and pain. Let your opponent graze your skin and you smash into his flesh; let him smash into your flesh and you fracture his bones; let him fracture your bones and you take his life! Do not be concerned with your escaping safely—lay your life before him!

The Game of Death (1972—released 1978)

Because Bruce Lee never lived to complete this film, we can only speculate as to what lessons he might have hoped to impart through it. Certainly none are present in the cut-and-paste film that was released under this title after his passing. We do know that he shot over one hour of footage. Sadly, only fifteen minutes showed up in the print that was released. Still, we can only smile when we ponder what might have been.

Lee had hoped to make this film the cinematic showcase for his martial philosophy of jeet kune do, and in this respect, it undoubtedly would have been brilliant. He wished to convey the ancient gung fu lesson of Yin/Yang, that teaches one the necessity of learning how to bend with adversity—not fight it head-on—and so survive. To learn how to instantly fill the gaps of an opponent's defense as they manifest and, like water, flow with every situation. (At the beginning of Chapter Six, we discussed what he had in mind for the opening scene of the film, which was never shot. We also talked about how he had hoped to evolve in his use of film as allegory in order to reveal

The Game of Death, *a film that was supposed to be about the principle of "bend and survive." Here Bruce Lee adapts himself to a rather large obstacle (in the form of Kareem Abdul-Jabbar) that besets him during preliminary fight-scene filming in October 1972.*

deeper spiritual truths through what, to the untrained eye, appear to be rather simple stories.)

Although Bruce Lee lived to complete only four films, you can see that in each one he attempted to communicate a moral, a lesson, a teaching that would impart something of lasting value to those who watched. It was this ability of Lee's that set him apart from every other martial artist and certainly what continues to set him apart from every martial artist who has attempted to replace him on the silver screen. He was a philosopher/teacher, and his life and vocation reflected his predilection.

Certainly the ability to honestly express himself came through in each and every one of his films. It was this potential of self-expression through cinematic allegory that attracted Lee to the profession in the first place. When asked by an American journalist if he enjoyed being an actor, Lee replied: *"Yes, every inch of it—because it is my way of expressing myself."*

Lee likened this process of honest self-expression to his great inner intensity (what I've chosen to call his inner warrior), and it was this basic, pure, and honest emotion that he expressed so convincingly through film that, according to Lee, was the main reason that audiences could relate to him:

> *I have this intensity in me that the audience believes in what I do because I believe in what I do. The intensity is there, and I have to act in such a way as to border my action somewhere between reality and fantasy. As long as what I do is credible and as long as I have this intensity in me, then all is well.*

While Bruce Lee is no longer with us to teach additional lessons, we are fortunate that through the written and recorded words he left behind and through his films, his teachings have endured. Despite his corporeal absence, Lee continues to instruct others with the same authority that he enjoyed throughout his brief life. There is every indication that Lee shall continue to instruct, inspire, and motivate entirely new generations of people toward their own method of personal liberation.

It is upon the shoulders of these individuals, those that may be partaking of his wisdom for the first time, that Bruce Lee's legacy shall be passed on to future generations.

CHAPTER SEVENTEEN

IN YOUR OWN PROCESS

aniel Inosanto, one of Lee's premiere disciples and the man that Lee himself chose to teach his martial art at Lee's third and final school in Los Angeles, has made some astute observations regarding some of the broader applications of Lee's martial philosophy. "Jeet kune do," he says, "was not an end in itself for Bruce, nor was it a mere byproduct of his martial studies; it was a means to self-discovery. JKD was a prescription for personal growth. It was an investigation of freedom—freedom to act naturally and effectively not only in combat, but in life. In life, we absorb what is useful and reject what is useless, and add to experience what is specifically our own."

Inosanto has been able to lead a fuller, more productive life as a result of applying Lee's JKD principles to his own day-to-day existence. But this isn't just a phenomenon reserved for upper-echelon martial artists such as Inosanto. As mentioned at the beginning of this book, people from all walks of life have been influenced by and benefited from Bruce Lee's philosophy and world view. To this end I enjoyed a recent conversation with Alex Ben Block apropos Lee's influence on his life. Block is the editor of the *Hollywood Reporter*. His interview with Lee in 1972 led to the first book written on Lee in this country, *The Legend of Bruce Lee*, which was published in 1974.

I asked Block what he had learned from his discussion with Lee. Block thought a moment and then answered: "Before I interviewed him I assumed that he was sort of the typical movie star type, that he was going to be some sort of glib guy who was shallow and without much depth. And in the short time I interviewed him, I realized that this was a man who had been down a difficult road, who had faced his share of prejudice, defeat, and difficulty, of troubled economic circumstances, and who was a man who really thought about things. He was a man who had a philosophy, and that philosophy came out of really thinking through, almost from the beginning, the process of his life. He was somebody who had said, 'You don't have to just take what comes along. You can go back and start with a blank sheet of paper and take something old and something new and something original and put it all together and interface those pieces to create something.' So I was quite impressed with him. And once I started seeing his films, I was even more impressed with him, because I realized that he was able to translate that art onto the screen."

Block went on to reveal that his life had, like Inosanto's, Ted Wong's, and the numerous other individuals with whom Lee had contact, been changed for the better by the experience: "It's hard to separate the interview I did from the research I did, from the book I wrote, to the experiences it has brought me, to the people I've met and been in touch with. I've been inspired by all of these, and I've learned from them. It's really touched my life in many, many different ways." Block's example is not unique, but it does serve to illustrate that Bruce Lee, and the philosophy that he espoused, have continued to endure and to influence people from all walks of life.

So what's in Bruce Lee's philosophy for you? That's a question only you can answer, and as you've read, it will depend, to a large part, on what you're seeking in your life.

Bruce Lee deliberately left behind no blueprint or one-size-fits-all system that was intended to be followed by one and all for the purpose of self-enlightenment, for the simple reason that self-enlightenment is just that—enlightenment of one's self. If you adopt somebody else's methods or copy their lifestyle, then you will only succeed in enlightening yourself as to what has proven effective for another person in their personal quest for truth.

If you truly understand what Bruce Lee's message was, then you will also realize that his way consists of no way. His method consists of no method. In fact, the logo Lee had designed for his art of jeet kune do contained the Chinese characters that expressed this very tenet of his philosophy: "Using no way as way; having no limitation as limitation."

At the foot of Bruce Lee's tombstone, in Lake View Cemetery, in Seattle, Washington, is this poignant—and very accurate—statement.

Bruce Lee's philosophy stressed that we should not be caught up in the traditions of the past at the expense of living the future properly. His philosophy incorporated taking the best of everything that pertained to one's particular mode of happiness, whether it was a beautiful sculpture or a beautiful poem—or even the joy to be derived from the practice of a given martial art or vocation—and learning how to synthesize this knowledge to make yourself a better, more productive individual, somebody who will leave his or her mark, in a positive, creative, and more productive way, on society—not because society "demands" it, but because it is in your true nature, or li, to do so.

Following what has been called "the Watercourse Way," or Tao, will prove to be a liberating process, with the result that you will live better, develop better interpersonal relationships, and learn and live by the virtues of honesty, integrity, and understanding that will enable all of us to get along and coexist in an ever more complex and difficult universe.

So what can you learn from the philosophy of Bruce Lee? Perhaps if you learn to apply the lessons found on these pages, you will see the universe and your role in it a little more clearly. You will wish neither to possess nor to be possessed. You will no longer covet paradise and no longer fear hell. And you will no longer judge people from a fixed position of prejudice. If you can overcome the obstacle of yourself, you will learn that you've had within you from the very beginning the medicine for your suffering. You will come to understand that you will never find your inner light unless, like the candle, you become your own fuel, consuming yourself.

Should you become discouraged during any part of your journey, simply recall the words of Bruce Lee from a letter he sent to one of his closest friends, Taky Kimura, after the latter had experienced a profound hardship:

> *Life is an ever-flowing process and somewhere on the path some unpleasant things will pop up—it might leave a scar—but then life is flowing on, and like running water, when it stops, it grows stale. Go bravely on, my friend, because each experience teaches us a lesson.*

And above all else, remember the lesson that Lee had hoped to impart to his son—a message of simplicity: *"Walk on."*

APPENDIXES

ECO-ZEN

by Alan Watts,
introduced by Mark Watts

*T*he integration of philosophy with martial arts, or more accurately, the leaving whole of something our cultural perspectives have divided, characterizes Bruce Lee's life work and carries his art forward. At the same time, however, reintegration takes us back to an almost forgotten ritual so notably missing in modern societies—the traditional rite of initiation into adulthood.

As practiced in most ancient cultures, this ritual invariably consisted of both physical and spiritual training, and the discipline was consummated in a trial or "vision quest" intended to test the worthiness of the initiate and to provide a galvanizing experience to, in effect, weld spirit with body for the journey through life. With this rite, individuals became responsible to the spirit and to the culture that lived by its law, variously called dharma, maat, me, rta, tao, *the dreaming, and the great spirit. Widespread interest in Far Eastern ways of liberation continues to grow because we recognize in these ways the ordinary wisdom of original peoples. [Note: this fascinating aspect of the martial arts as rite of passage is brought fully to light in the essay "The Tao of Wu-hsin," which was transcribed from a talk that was given by my father in the early 1960s and appears for the first time in this book.]*

Today one of the brightest rays of hope that humans will once again realize completeness and reintegrate into nature comes with the historic Western interest in Eastern thought. It is possible that an awakening to the reality of an integrated systems view of the world will increase the development of sustainable technologies, which, in turn, will make their way to the rapidly growing industrial base of the East. Our best bet is that this process will take root before the view of separateness allows irrec-

oncilable actions to upset the balance of organism and environment upon which the survival of all life depends.

My father addressed this need in "Eco-Zen" (a chapter from his book The Philosophies of Asia)*, which is reprinted here in part.*

∞

When a scientist starts carefully paying attention to the behavior of people and things, he discovers that they go together, and that the behavior of the organism is inseparable from the behavior of its environment. We have come to think that the figure exists independently of the background, but actually they go together just as inseparably as backs go with fronts, as positives go with negatives, as ups go with downs and as life goes with death. You cannot separate it. So, there is a sort of secret conspiracy between the figure and the background: they are really one, but they look different. They need each other, just as male needs female and vice versa. But we are, ordinarily, completely unaware of this. And so, the biologist comes to say that what he is describing is no longer merely the organism and its behavior. He is describing a field which he now calls the "organism/environment," and that field is what the individual actually is. Now, this is very clearly recognized in all sorts of sciences, but the average individual, and indeed the average scientist, does not feel in a way that corresponds to his theory. He still feels as if he were a center of sensitivity locked up inside a bag of skin.

The object of Buddhist discipline, or methods of psychological training, is, as it were, to turn that feeling inside out; to bring about a state of affairs in which the individual feels himself to be everything that there is. The whole cosmos is focused, expressing itself here, and you are the whole cosmos expressing itself there, and there, and there and there and so on. In other words, the reality of my self fundamentally is not something inside my skin, but everything, and I mean everything, outside my skin, but doing what is my skin and inside it. In the same way, when the ocean has a wave on it, the wave is not separate from the ocean. Every wave on the ocean is the whole ocean *wav-ing*. The ocean *waves*, and it says, "Yoo-hoo—I'm here! I can wave in many different ways, I can wave this way and that way." And so, the "ocean of being" *waves* every one of us, and we are its waves, but the wave is fundamentally the ocean.

Now, in that way, your sense of identity would be turned inside out. You wouldn't forget who you were—your name and address, your telephone number, your social security number and what sort of role you are supposed to occupy in society. But you would know that this particular role that you play and this particular personality that you are is superficial, and the real you is all that there is. The inversion, or, turning upside down of the sense of identity, of the state of consciousness which the average person has, is the objective of Buddhist disciplines.

Now, I think that this is something of very great importance to the Western world today. We have developed an immensely powerful technology. We have stronger means of changing the physical universe than has ever existed before. How are we going to use it? A Chinese proverb says that if the wrong man uses the right means, the right means works in the wrong way. Let us assume that our technological knowledge is the right means. What kind of people are going to use this knowledge? Are they going to be people who hate nature and feel alienated from it, or people who love the physical world and feel that the physical world is their own personal body?

The whole attitude of using technology as a method of fighting the world will succeed only in destroying the world, as we are doing. We use absurd, and uninformed and short-sighted methods of getting rid of insect pests, forcing our fruit and tomatoes to grow, stripping our hills of trees and so on, thinking that this is some kind of progress. Actually, it is turning everything into a junk heap. It is said that Americans, who are in the forefront of technological progress, are materialists. Nothing is further from the truth.

American culture is dedicated to the hatred of material and to its transformation into junk. Look at our cities. Do they look as though they were made by people who love material? Everything is made out of ticky-tacky, which is a combination of plaster of paris, papier-mâché and plastic glue—and it comes in any flavor.

The important lesson is that technology and its powers must be handled by true materialists. True materialists are people who love material—who cherish wood and stone and wheat and eggs and animals and above all, the earth—and treat it with a reverence that is due one's own body.

(This essay is used with permission from Mark Watts and Tuttle Publishing, from the book *The Philosophies of Asia*, Tuttle Publishing, Boston, 1995.)

THE TAO OF WU-HSIN

by Alan Watts

Perhaps one of the best ways of demonstrating the meaning of what the Chinese call wu-hsin, or the Japanese mushin (a non-fixated mind), is through the application of Zen to the Japanese martial art of fencing. As some of you may be aware, Japanese fencing, or kendo, translates as "the way of the sword." It is an art that is performed with gruesome-looking swords and the samurai, or Japanese feudal soldiery, used to practice Zen to give them courage, and they applied it to the art of fencing.

Now if you are ever given to study with a Japanese fencing master, you will not at first be given a sword and be told how to use it. You will instead be made a kind of janitor around the house. You will have to do all the little chores like sweeping the floors, putting away the bedding, washing up the dishes, and so on and so forth. And while you are doing all of that, the master will get hold of a practice sword called a *shinai*, the blade of which is made up of about six strips of bamboo loosely tied together, and if you get hit with it—although it may give you a pretty hard crack—at least you won't get killed! However, while the poor boy who is the apprentice is doing the household duties, the teacher stalks around with one of these things and, unawares, gives the apprentice a bang on the head!

The boy is expected to defend himself by any means at his disposal: If he's got a saucepan in hand, he's expected to use the saucepan. If he's in the midst of picking up a cushion, then he is expected to use the cushion. And everywhere, always at unknown moments, the teacher sneaks up on him and bangs him on the head. After a while, the poor fellow is going around looking this way and that, expecting at any moment the teacher to hit him, and he begins in his mind to plan how he can be ready to meet the teacher's assault. If, for example, he's going along a passage, he's expecting the teacher to come right round the corner at the end, and instead of that, just as he's all ready to defend himself to the front—Doing!—he gets hit on the head from behind.

Now when this has been going on for a little time, there are only two possibilities: the apprentice either has a nervous breakdown and quits—or he *learns*.

And what does he learn? He learns that the teacher will always outwit him. That he can never be prepared for an unexpected attack, and so he gives up trying to *control* the situation. He gives up trying to prepare. In other words, he just wanders around with an attitude of, "Well, maybe I'll get hit or maybe I won't." He gives up *caring* whether he gets hit or not and—at that moment—the teacher gives him the practice sword and says, "Now you can begin to learn fencing."

The importance of this is simply that if, say, you are faced with a group of attackers and you don't know from where the next attack is going to come, if you attempt to *pre-prepare*, or get ready to go for one fellow, you might find, all of a sudden, that you have to deal with another one who is coming for you. All of your preparation has been for naught, as you now have to withdraw from the first plan of counterattack in order to deal with the second one. But if you're in a middle or *noncommitted* position, and you're not tensed in mind in any *particular* direction, then you are ready to go in all directions, wherever the attack may come from.

And so in exactly the same way the Zen way of teaching teaches one to see that you cannot—cannot—be in *complete control* of your whole life situation. You cannot, in other words, fundamentally *possess* yourself.

BRUCE LEE'S PRINCIPAL WORKS

1940–1958. Appears in no less than twenty childhood films. His first (at the age of three months) is shot in San Francisco and entitled *Golden Gate Girl*. Other titles include *The Birth of Mankind* (shot in 1946), *My Son, Ah Cheung*, *It's Father's Fault*, *The Thunderstorm*, and his last childhood film, *The Orphan*, which is shot in Hong Kong in 1958.

1963. Writes and self-publishes a book on the art of gung fu entitled *Chinese Gung Fu: The Philosophical Art of Self-Defense*. Only five hundred copies of the original book are printed.

September 9, 1966–July 14, 1967. Stars in *The Green Hornet* television series. He films twenty-six episodes that air on Friday from 7:30 to 8:00 P.M. on ABC-TV.

January 27, 1967. Appears as Kato in a two-part episode ABC-TV series *Batman*.

July 14, 1967. Shoots an episode of the television series *Ironside*.

July 5, 1968. Works as the technical director for the film *The Wrecking Crew*, a campy spy spoof starring Dean Martin as special agent Matt Helm.

August 1, 1968. Films the movie *Marlowe* at MGM. Originally entitled *Little Sister*, the film was based on Raymond Chandler's novel *The Little Sister*. It starred James Garner as Philip Márlowe and featured a spectacular scene in which Lee walks in and single-handedly destroys Garner's office, including a chandelier, which he smashes with an eight-foot vertical kick.

November 12, 1968. Films an episode of the television series *Blondie* for Universal.

November 15–22, 1968. Films an episode of the television series *Here Come the Brides* for Screen Gems. The title of this episode is "Marriage, Chinese Style," in which Lee has a major supporting role and appears as a non–martial artist.

April 16–24, 1969. Works as the technical director for a fight scene for the climax of the Columbia Pictures film *A Walk in the Spring Rain*.

June 24–July 1, 1971. Films the premiere episode of the television series *Longstreet*. The script is written by Lee and his student Stirling Silliphant and features Lee teaching James Franciscus his personal art of jeet kune do.

July 12, 1971. Leaves for Pak Chong, Thailand, to film *The Big Boss* for Golden Harvest Films. He returns to Los Angeles on September 6, 1971. The film firmly establishes Bruce Lee as an electrifying movie presence, smashing the all-time box office record in Hong Kong.

July 7, 1971. Films three additional episodes of *Longstreet*, entitled "Spell Legacy of Death," "Wednesday's Child," and "I See, Said the Blind Man."

November 9, 1971. Sits for interview by Pierre Berton in what has since become known as *The Lost Interview*. It is Lee's only surviving video interview.

1971. Completes his second film for Golden Harvest, entitled *Fists of Fury*. It smashes the record set by *The Big Boss*, and Bruce becomes a national hero.

1972. Forms his own production company, Concord Productions, with Golden Harvest founder, Raymond Chow. Lee leaves for Rome to film *The Way of the Dragon*. It costars Chuck Norris. (Lee had also given Chuck work during the filming of *The Wrecking Crew*.) This film again sets a new box office record.

1972. Begins filming the fight sequences for a philosophical/martial arts film called *The Game of Death*. But filming is interrupted so that Lee can begin filming his next picture, a joint production by Sequoia and Concord for Warner Brothers.

1973. Films *Enter the Dragon*, which is still considered the classic of the martial arts genre.

July 20, 1973. Passes away in Hong Kong.

August 1973. *Enter the Dragon* premieres to enthusiastic worldwide response. Though released in August, *Enter the Dragon* goes on to outgross all other films that year except *The Exorcist*. Made for only $500,000, it has, to date, brought in over $300,000,000.

1974. A little over one year after Lee's death, a compilation of three episodes of *The Green Hornet* are spliced together and released theatrically.

1975. Linda Lee publishes some of her husband's notes on combat principles, theory, and philosophy. The book is entitled *The Tao of Jeet Kune Do*.

Fall 1978. Lee's last film, *Game of Death*, is rewritten and completed with a stand-in and cardboard cutouts of Bruce Lee. It is poorly edited, and despite Lee's having filmed over an hour's worth of footage, only fifteen minutes of it is included in the film. The sloppy editing and inferior stand-ins all but ruin the film's continuity. While marketed as a "tribute to Bruce Lee," it sadly is not. Still, on the strength of his name, it goes on to gross over $300,000,000 worldwide.

November 1993. Bruce Lee's video interview with Pierre Berton is discovered perfectly intact in the Canadian broadcasting archives. It is released shortly thereafter as *Bruce Lee: The Lost Interview*. It is immediately hailed as a historical triumph by Bruce Lee fans across the globe and is considered to be one of the most riveting films of Bruce Lee in existence, featuring Lee at his charismatic best, simply being himself, rather than acting or playing a character.

CHRONOLOGY OF THE LIFE OF BRUCE LEE

November 27, 1940. *San Francisco.* Born in the "hour of the Dragon" (between 6:00 and 8:00 A.M.) at Jackson Street Hospital in Chinatown, the son of Mr. and Mrs. Lee Hoi Chuen. His mother christened him Lee Jun Fan ("Return Again"), believing that he would one day return to live in the United States. He is renamed Bruce by a nurse at the hospital. Eventually, he acquires the nickname Sai Fon ("Small Phoenix"), a feminine name. (His parents, following Chinese tradition when sons are born, address him by a girl's name in order to confuse the spirits who might steal away his soul.)

February 1941. *San Francisco.* Appears in his first film at the age of three months. He is soon given the nickname Mo Si Tung (Never Sits Still).

1946. *Hong Kong.* Appears in his first "real" film, *The Beginning of a Boy*. He is six years old. At eight years of age, he makes his second film. This film marks the first time that he goes by the name Lee Siu Lung (Lee Little Dragon)—the name by which he would later become famous in Hong Kong and all the Mandarin film theaters throughout Southeast Asia. All told, he will appear in over twenty films before the age of eighteen in Hong Kong. His last film as a child star is called *The Orphan*.

1953. *Hong Kong.* Enters La Salle College after attending Chinese elementary schools. Lee is easily bored by the formality of this Catholic high school (which his son, Brandon, would also later attend), and despite his keen mind, his grades suffer as a result. His favorite after-school activity is getting into scraps with the British boys.

1953. *Hong Kong.* Takes up the Wing Chun style of gung fu under master martial artist Yip Man after claiming to have been "bullied" at school. His mother pays the going rate of twelve Hong Kong dollars per lesson. Lee also has his first run-in with the Triads, or Chinese Mafia, when he decks the son of one their leaders, to whom he refuses to bow down. His constant fighting begins to concern his mother and father.

1958. *Hong Kong.* Recognized as the "Crown Colony Cha-Cha Champion" at the age of eighteen. He keeps a list of 108 different dance steps on a card in his wallet.

March 29, 1958. *Hong Kong.* Moves on to St. Francis Xavier after being "asked" to leave La Salle College. At Xavier, Lee is convinced to enter the interschool boxing competition by Brother Kenny. Utilizing a mixture of western boxing and Wing Chun, Lee soundly defeats the three-year defending champion, Gary Elm of St. George V School.

April 29, 1959. *Hong Kong.* Accepts a challenge from members of a rival gung fu school to fight on a Hong Kong rooftop. While removing his jacket, Lee is sucker-punched and goes into a rage, knocking his opponent cold and dislodging a tooth. The boy's parents complain to the authorities. Lee's father, Lee Hoi Chuen, now enters the picture, and it is decided that the boy should return to San Francisco.

May 17, 1959. *San Francisco.* Arrives in San Francisco for the first time since his birth there eighteen years ago (he teaches cha-cha on the voyage from Hong Kong). The trip, lasting some eighteen days, proves a period of deep introspection and readjustment.

September 3, 1959. *Seattle.* Arrives in Seattle for the first time. Soon after, Lee enrolls in Edison Technical School (fall quarter) to complete his secondary school education. He soon gains a following among several students at Edison after they see him in action at Seattle's Seafair pageant.

1960. *Seattle.* Challenged by a black belt karate man from Japan. During one of his early demonstrations, Lee's views on martial arts are attacked by the man, and after initially ignoring the challenges, Lee loses his patience and agrees to fight the man "with no rules" at the local YMCA. The fight lasts only eleven seconds and ends when Lee straight-punches the man the length of the gymnasium. The man asks to become his student.

December 1960. *Seattle.* Graduates from Edison Technical School.

March 27, 1961. *Seattle.* Enrolls at the University of Washington (spring quarter). Shortly thereafter, he meets seventeen-year-old Linda Emery, who would later become his wife, and majors in philosophy. He lectures on gung fu and Chinese philosophy and self-publishes his first book, *Chinese Gung Fu, the Philosophical Art of Self-Defense.*

March 26, 1963. *Seattle.* Departs for Hong Kong after spending four years in the United States.

August 1963. *Seattle.* Returns from Hong Kong.

1964. *Seattle.* Leaves the University of Washington after spring quarter.

July 19, 1964. *Seattle.* Departs for Oakland, California.

August 3, 1964. *Oakland.* Begins teaching gung fu in Oakland.

August 17, 1964. *Seattle.* Marries Linda Emery.

1964. *Oakland.* Challenged by one of the top martial artists in the Chinese community for teaching Chinese martial arts to Caucasians. Though Lee subdues him in three minutes, he's annoyed at how long it took him and how tired he felt afterward. He begins to reexamine his "traditional" approach to the martial arts.

August 2, 1964. *Long Beach, California.* Performs a demonstration at Ed Parker's Long Beach International Karate Tournament. His exhibition is filmed by Parker, who gives the tape to Jay Sebring, the hairstylist for *Batman* producer William Dozier, who is looking to cast a part in a new TV pilot, "Number One Son." Lee is given a screen test by 20th Century–Fox, but the show never airs.

1965. *Los Angeles*. Paid $1,800 by Dozier as a retainer for his services until *The Green Hornet* is ready to shoot the next year.

February 1, 1965. *Oakland*. Becomes a father when Linda gives birth to their son, Brandon Bruce, whom Lee describes as "the only blond-haired, blue-eyed Chinaman in California."

February 8, 1965. *Hong Kong*. Lee's father passes away.

July 1965. *Hong Kong*. Takes his young son with him to Hong Kong to visit his family. While there, he begins to seriously expand his martial arts perspective, laying the conceptual groundwork for what will eventually become a revolutionary approach to the martial arts, jeet kune do.

June 6, 1966. *Hollywood*. Begins filming on a new TV series entitled *The Green Hornet*. Bruce makes his television debut as Kato, the Green Hornet's valet and chauffeur. He receives tons of fan mail and is a megahit with children across the United States, but the show is canceled after only one season.

February 5, 1967. *Los Angeles*. Starts the Jun Fan Gung Fu Institute in Chinatown.

May 6, 1967. *Washington, D.C.* Performs at the National Karate Championship.

June 24, 1967. *New York*. Appears at the All-American Open Karate Championship at Madison Square Garden.

July 30, 1967. *Long Beach, California*. Attends Long Beach International Karate Tournament.

March 1968. *Los Angeles*. Begins giving private lessons. Some of his students are celebrities, whom he charges $250 an hour. His student list reads like a Los Angeles Who's Who: Steve McQueen, James Coburn, Lee Marvin, James Garner, Kareem Abdul-Jabbar, screenwriter Sterling Silliphant, and director Roman Polanski.

1968. *Los Angeles.* Finds work as the technical director for the movie *The Wrecking Crew.*

1968. *Los Angeles.* Begins to complete the conceptual framework of his philosophy of martial arts, which he labels "jeet kune do," or in English, "the way of the intercepting fist." It stresses economy of motion and freedom of martial expression.

1968–69. *Hollywood.* Lands occasional roles in film and television productions, including *Blondie, Here Come the Brides,* and *Marlowe,* but racism in Hollywood prevents Lee from attaining the kind of success he's confident he can achieve.

April 19, 1969. *Santa Monica.* Bruce and Linda's daughter, Shannon, is born.

1969–70. *Hollywood.* Works with Sterling Silliphant and James Coburn on a script entitled *The Silent Flute,* based on Bruce's martial arts philosophy. The project eventually goes south when Warner Brothers decides that they'll finance it only if it's shot in India (where they have some money tied up). Unfortunately, the locale doesn't coincide with the concept shared by Silliphant and Coburn, and they pull out of the project.

June 27, 1971. *Los Angeles.* Appears in screenwriter Sterling Silliphant's one hour TV pilot for Paramount Pictures' *Longstreet.* The episode is called "The Way of the Intercepting Fist" (i.e., jeet kune do) and Lee plays a supporting role as Longstreet's martial arts instructor. The audience response to Lee's character is so strong that Paramount writes him into three more episodes and considers creating a series exclusively for Bruce to star in.

1971. *Los Angeles.* Meets Fred Weintraub and plans begin to develop a concept for a TV series called *The Warrior* (later renamed *Kung Fu*). Lee decides to pursue some options in Hong Kong.

1971. *Hong Kong.* Arrives in Hong Kong an unsuspecting superstar, thanks to Hong Kong reruns of *The Green Hornet*, which is highly popular. Raymond Chow, the owner of a new production company, attempts to recruit Lee to star in one of his films. He offers Lee the lead role in a film called *The Big Boss.*

July 1971. *Thailand.* Sets to work to film *The Big Boss* (released in the United States as *Fists of Fury*). Made for a mere $100,000 in Pak Chong, Thailand, the film opens in Hong Kong to ecstatic reviews and fan turnout. It grosses a record $3.2 million in its first run.

December 7, 1971. Receives official word that the lead role in *The Warrior* TV series has been given to dancer/actor David Carradine because Hollywood producers believe Bruce is too Chinese-looking to star in a Western TV series.

December 9, 1971. *Hong Kong.* Records his historic *Lost Interview* with Canadian journalist Pierre Berton. It is the only time he speaks for a full half-hour about his life, art, and career. After airing one time in Ontario, Canada, the tape of the interview is believed to have been destroyed.

1972. *Hong Kong.* Lee's second film, *Fist of Fury* (released in the United States as *The Chinese Connection*), is made for $200,000 and breaks all records set by *The Big Boss*. In Singapore, scalpers get $45 for a $2 ticket and the film has to be withdrawn to ease traffic jams. In the Philippines, it's shut down to give domestic films a chance. Eventually, both of Lee's first two films gross over $20 million.

1972. *Hong Kong.* Rejects director Lo Wei's script for *Yellow-Faced Tiger* in favor of one he creates, writes, directs, stars in, and tentatively titles *Enter the Dragon*. This becomes his third film, *The Way of the Dragon* (released in the United States after Lee's death as *Return of the Dragon*). The film again shatters all previous box office records in Hong Kong.

1972. *Hong Kong.* Bruce Lee announces that his next project will be called *Game of Death* and will feature the greatest martial arts masters in the world. He begins preliminary work on the film and records several fight scenes, including one with NBA superstar Kareem Abdul-Jabbar.

1972. *Hollywood.* Lee signs a big deal with Warner Brothers to film *Enter the Dragon,* the first-ever production between the United States and Hong Kong film industries, before *Game of Death* can be completed.

February 1973. *Hong Kong.* Begins production of *Enter the Dragon*. Lee is now mobbed wherever he goes in public and also receives challenges like a latter-day Billy the Kid from martial artists looking to make a name for themselves. He ignores most of these challenges but, when pressed to take it further, mops the floor with his adversaries.

April 1973. *Hong Kong.* Completes *Enter the Dragon*. At a special prerelease screening (no music or special effects had been added at this point), Lee realizes that this is the film that will make him an international star.

May 10, 1973. *Hong Kong.* Collapses during a dubbing session for *Enter the Dragon*. He convulses and loses consciousness. He is immediately rushed by ambulance to the hospital, where the doctors detect major brain swelling and prescribe drugs to reduce it. Lee then flies to California to be checked out by a medical team at UCLA. They declare him in perfect health with "the body of an 18-year-old."

July 20, 1973. *Hong Kong.* Dies as the result of a cerebral edema, cause of death is cited as "misadventure." An instantaneous swelling of his brain is believed to have been brought on by an allergic reaction to a combination of meprobamate (a pain-killing ingredient found in medication for his lower-back pain) and an aspirinlike headache tablet called Equagesic.

July 25, 1973. *Hong Kong.* A symbolic funeral is held for Bruce for the benefit of his family, friends, and fans. Over 25,000 people jam Kowloon during his funeral service.

July 31, 1973. *Seattle.* Laid to rest in Lake View Cemetery. His pallbearers are friends and students Steve McQueen, James Coburn, Danny Inosanto, Peter Chin, Taky Kimura, and his brother, Robert Lee.

REFERENCES

Preface
1. William James, *The Writings of William James*, ed. John J. McDermott, (Chicago: University of Chicago Press, 1977).
2. Kareem Abdul-Jabbar (with Peter Knobler), *Giant Steps* (New York: Bantam Books, 1983).

Chapter 2
1. Ludwig Wittgenstein, *Tractatus Logico-Philosophicus,* trans. D. F. Pears and B. P. McGuiness (New York: Routledge and Kegan Paul, Ltd., 1974).
2. Lao-tzu, *Tao te ching*, trans. Stephen Mitchell (New York: HarperCollins, 1988).

Chapter 3
1. Wing-Tsit Chan, ed. and trans., *A Sourcebook In Chinese Philosophy* (New Jersey: Princeton University Press, 1963).
2. Charles M. Blakewell, ed., *Sourcebook in Ancient Philosophy* (New York: Charles Scribner's Sons, 1909).
3. Alan W. Watts, *The Way of Zen* (New York: Pantheon, 1957).
4. Daisetz T. Suzuki, *Zen and Japanese Culture* (New York: Princeton University Press, 1959).
5. Lao-tzu, *Tao te ching*.
6. Alan W. Watts, *The Way of Zen*.

Chapter 4
1. Wing-Tsit Chan, ed. and trans., *A Sourcebook In Chinese Philosophy*.
2. Charles M. Blakewell, ed., *Sourcebook in Ancient Philosophy*.
3. Lao-tzu, *Tao te ching*.
4. Ibid.

Chapter 5
1. Fun Yu-lan, *A History of Chinese Philosophy,* trans. Derk Bodde (London: Princeton University Press and George Allen & Unwin, 1952).

2. Chuang-tzu, *The Way of Chuang-tzu*, trans. Thomas Merton (Boston and London: Shambhala, 1992).

3. Lao-tzu, *The Way of Life*, trans. R. B. Blakney (New York: Penguin Books, 1983).

Chapter 6

1. Alan W. Watts, *Tao: the Watercourse Way* (New York: Quality Paperback Book Club, 1994).

2. Alan W. Watts, *The Way of Zen*.

3. Lin Yutang, ed. and trans., *The Wisdom of Lao-tse* (New York: Modern Library, 1948).

4. Lucien Stryk, ed., *Zen: Poems, Prayers, Sermons, Anecdotes, Interviews* (New York: Doubleday, 1963).

Chapter 7

1. Lao-tzu, *Tao te ching*.

2. Ibid.

3. Will Durant, *The Mansions of Philosophy* (New York: Simon & Schuster, 1929).

4. Johann Wolfgang Goethe, *Selected Verse*, ed. and trans. David Luke (New York: Penguin, 1964).

5. Lucien Stryk, ed., *Zen: Poems, Prayers, Sermons, Anecdotes, Interviews*.

6. Lao-tzu, *Tao te ching*.

7. Will Durant, *The Mansions of Philosophy*.

Chapter 8

1. Will and Ariel Durant, *The Lessons of History* (New York: Simon & Schuster, 1968).

2. Alan W. Watts, *This Is It* (New York: Vintage Books, 1973).

Chapter 11

1. Wing-Tsit Chan, ed. and trans., *A Sourcebook In Chinese Philosophy*.

2. Deepak Chopra, M.D., *Ageless Body, Timeless Mind* (New York: Harmony Books, 1991).

Chapter 12

1. Lao-tzu, *Tao te ching*.

Chapter 14

1. Wing-Tsit Chan, ed. and trans., *A Sourcebook In Chinese Philosophy*.

FOR FURTHER RESEARCH

*I*n order to learn more about the philosophy of Bruce Lee and its many applications, the following audiocassettes, videos, and books are recommended.

Audio Recordings

The Warrior Within. This unabridged audio adaptation of the book is narrated by the author and features rare recordings of Bruce Lee and Brandon Lee speaking on key philosophical points covered in the text. This multitape set also includes additional material providing more depth on specific topics and an interview with the author. (Price: $39.95 plus $4 shipping. Send orders to PFP Direct, 10400 Overland Road, Suite 251, Boise, ID 83709. For credit-card orders, the 24-hour number is [800] 362-9886.)

The Bruce Lee Audio Series features the only firsthand recordings of Bruce Lee in existence. This four-volume series offers a fascinating opportunity for listeners to experience Bruce Lee and his teachings directly from the man himself:

Volume I. *Bruce Lee: The Lost Interview.* This is the complete interview. Plus, exclusively on this audiocassette, Pierre Berton, the man who conducted this historic interview, offers his own insight into its origins, its impact, and the significance of Bruce Lee. (Price: $12.95; California residents add $1.07 sales tax.)

Volume II. *Bruce Lee: The Alex Ben Block Interview.* This telephone interview conducted by *Hollywood Reporter* editor Alex Ben Block would later be the basis for the first-ever biography of Bruce Lee in North America, *The Legend of Bruce Lee.* Lee speaks in great detail about his life, success, and how he was adjusting to superstardom. On side B, Block recollects the history of the interview and assesses the significance of Lee's films and philosophy. (Price: $12.95; California residents add $1.07 sales tax.)

Volume III. *Bruce Lee: The Ted Thomas Interview.* Almost every biography on Bruce Lee has quoted from this comprehensive interview with British broadcaster Ted Thomas during a Radio Hong Kong interview that aired in 1971. Lee discusses his friendship with celebrity students Steve McQueen and James Coburn, his appearance as Kato on *The Green Hornet* TV series, his own unique approach to combat, and many other issues bearing on his life and career. On side B, Thomas recalls knowing Bruce Lee during his superstar years in Hong Kong. (Price: $12.95; California residents add $1.07 sales tax.)

Volume IV. *The Bruce Lee Sampler.* This special tape consists of excerpts from volumes I through III in The Bruce Lee Audio Series. It also includes a bonus recording of Bruce Lee's approach to combat not heard anywhere else in the series. Highly recommended for first-time listeners. (Price: $7.95; California residents add $.65 sales tax.)

Books

Bruce Lee: The Lost Interview. Lee's most famous interview in handy-to-reference book form. (Price: $6.95; California residents add $.57 sales tax.)

Tao of Jeet Kune Do, by Bruce Lee. This international bestseller explains the philosophical basis of jeet kune do in Lee's original words and drawings, as excerpted from his diary and notes after his death. Lee's views on Zen, physical training, combat, martial virtues and failings, and many other topics are presented. (ISBN: 0-89750-048-2. Ohara Publications, Inc., P.O. Box 918, Santa Clarita, CA 91380; [800] 423-2874. Order code no. 401.)

Videotapes

Bruce Lee: The Lost Interview. Described by friends, family, and students as "vintage Bruce," this is Lee's only surviving video interview. It features twenty-five minutes of uninterrupted dialogue between Lee and Canadian journalist Pierre Berton. (Price: $19.95; California residents add $1.64 sales tax.)

Bruce Lee's Jeet Kune Do. This film is a wonderful introduction to Bruce Lee's martial art of jeet kune do. Lee personally explains and demonstrates his punching method, his kicking techniques, his movement and combat principles, and the key tenets of his philosophy of combat. It is narrated by Lee himself, with additional commentary provided by Brandon Lee and Dan Inosanto. Also included are many of Lee's personal research notes, drawings, home movies, private videos, and audio recordings. (Price: $39.95 plus $3.00 shipping and handling. Address: Legacy Productions USA L.C., c/o Little-Wolff Creative Group, 26500 West Agoura Road, Suite 502, Calabasas, CA 91302.)

To order *Bruce Lee: The Lost Interview*—book or video—or any or all four volumes of the Bruce Lee Audio Series, send a certified check or money order (U.S. funds only) to Little-Wolff Creative Group, 26500 West Agoura Road, Suite 502, Calabasas, CA 91302. For credit-card orders, call Little-Wolff's 24-hour number: (800) 64-BRUCE.

Also Recommended

As Alan Watts proved a significant influence on Bruce Lee, I am only too pleased to recommend the series of Alan Watts audio lectures available from Electronic University. For information, please write to Electronic University, P.O. Box 2309, San Anselmo, CA 94979, or call (800) 969-2887.

Proceeds derived from the sales of all books, videos, and audiocassettes will go to benefit both the Bruce Lee and Brandon Lee Medical Scholarship Endowment at the University of Arkansas and the Brandon Lee Drama Scholarship at Whitman College, in Walla Walla, Washington. If you would like to make your own contributions to these two worthy causes, we encourage you to please write or call:

The University of Arkansas
4301 West Markham, #716
Little Rock, AR 72205-7199
(501) 686-7950

Whitman College
Development Office
Walla Walla, WA 99362
(509) 527-5165

ABOUT THE AUTHOR

*J*ohn Little is uniquely suited to the task of relating the philosophy of Bruce Lee and his approach to life. Little has a degree in philosophy from McMaster University in Hamilton, Ontario, Canada, is the coauthor of two books on health and fitness (having spent over fifteen years as a writer for several fitness magazines), and is himself a student of Lee's art of jeet kune do.

Selected by the Bruce Lee estate, Little is the only person who has ever been authorized to review the entirety of Lee's personal notes, sketches, and reading annotations and to edit books on the subject of Lee's martial art and its far-reaching philosophical underpinnings. Little's keen awareness of the subtleties of both Eastern and Western philosophy coupled with a respect for the preservation of the essence of Lee's words and meaning give this book an integrity that is all too rare.

INDEX